Other Books by Adelaide Bry

Inside Psychotherapy

The T.A. Primer

The Sexually Aggressive Woman

T.A. Games

T.A. for Families

est: 60 Hours That Transform Your Life

Directing the Movies of Your Mind

GETTING BETTER

GETTING BETTER

BY ADELAIDE BRY

Rawson, Wade Publishers, Inc.
New York

Library of Congress Cataloging in Publication Data

Bry, Adelaide.
Getting better.

Includes index.
1. Psychotherapy. 2. Consumer education. I. Title.
RC480.5.B767 1978 616.8′914 78–55608
ISBN 0–89256–044–4
LC 78–55608

Published simultaneously in Canada by
McClelland and Stewart, Ltd.
Manufactured in the United States of America
by The Book Press, Brattleboro, Vermont

Designed by Joyce C. Weston
First Edition

To my dear friend
Dr. J. Herbert Hamsher

CONTENTS

With grateful acknowledgment to Laura Hobe, whose assistance in writing this book has been invaluable to me

GETTING BETTER

FIRST...

"Adelaide, I need help!"

They were familiar words, as any psychotherapist can tell you. But I hardly expected to hear them spoken by my very good friend, who seemed to be a together person.

"Okay," I said. "What kind of help?"

"That's just the problem—I don't know." Shelley burst into tears of frustration. It was some time before she recovered enough to begin at the beginning.

Shelley's problem was that she really didn't know what her problem was. Like a lot of other people who come to my office, she was doing okay financially, okay in her job, okay in her love life, with her family, her friends, but somehow not quite okay all the way.

"Something's missing," Shelley said. "It's as if I were a great big fantastic jigsaw puzzle that was all finished—except for one missing piece. I don't know what that piece is, or where to find it, but I'm not right without it. Do you know what I mean?"

I did. Shelley wasn't a greedy person. She wasn't insisting on getting everything in life. She simply wanted to be her whole and complete self. Now how could I argue with that? It's what everyone has a right to be—but hardly ever is.

"You do need help," I said.

Shelley threw up her hands in despair. "Now we're back to square one—*what kind?* Adelaide, there are so many different kinds of help—how can I know which one to choose?"

And there she had me.

There are therapies and techniques and programs and systems and mind sets and philosophies galore. Each one makes its claims and each one is different from the others. Undoubtedly each one offers genuine help for the person in need—but in need of what? How is the average person supposed to know which one offers the specific kind of help he needs, especially if he doesn't know exactly what his problem is?

Suppose a person has a vague feeling of incompleteness, like my friend Shelley. Should she be psychoanalyzed, behaviorally modified, psychosynthesized, Rolfed, meditated, biofeedbacked, Primal Screamed, hypnotized, megavitamined, assertiveness trained, ested, Masters-and-Johnsoned, or Aricaed, to name only some of the choices before her? And how can a person make a choice without knowing what is involved in each one of these possibilities? Or how much time they require?

Then there's the problem of the problem

Exactly.

Even if a person goes to all the trouble of finding out what is involved in each therapeutic possibility, what then? Suppose he isn't sure what is bothering him? How can he find out? Or at least get a clue?

And—

Suppose a person does have a clue to what ails her. How can she decide which kind of help is best for her particular kind of problem?

As Shelley said, back to square one.

And then I said . . .

"Not necessarily."

I had made my decision. I was going to write a book describing the many different kinds of help a person can get today. I was familiar with them, both personally and professionally. I had experienced many of them and had already written exhaustively on a few of them. But it was Shelley, and all the other Shelleys in the world, who needed the information I had in my notes and in my head. Then she, and they, could make their own choices about which kind of therapy was right.

To help them make these choices, I would also include a description of twelve problems I consider to be our most common afflictions today. Then, if the clue fits . . .

So there we have the therapies and the problems. Then what? my friend Shelley would say. And she's right. We have to match the therapies with the problems, which is exactly what I will do—or, rather, what I will allow the therapies themselves to do, because each one does aim at a specific type of problem or area of development. No one claims to be right for all persons and all needs. The individual's own personality also has to be considered. Not everyone would like psychoanalysis, TM, est, etc.

It would be impossible to include *all* available therapies in our current society. The book would just be too big. So I would include those that are available to most people in most areas of the country. Unavoidably, however, the list is a little subjective. Any list compiled by a person, or persons, has to be.

In most instances I have tried to give the reader some idea of what a therapy or procedure will cost and how much time will be involved, but these figures must, of necessity, be general rather than exact. The amount of time a method of therapy requires depends a great deal upon the person, the problem, the goal, and the therapist. Therefore I can indicate only an average, based upon the experience of the therapists involved, and in some instances that information cannot be estimated.

So far as costs are concerned, I am almost reluctant to include them because 1) they vary from therapist to therapist and from one part of the country to another, and 2) by the time of publication the current rate of inflation will have changed the costs. Consequently I am offering a range—and a wide one—of fees charged, in the hope that they will at least give the reader some idea of what he can afford.

For the health of it

Then I had another thought. Suppose Shelley finds something helpful in *all* the therapies in this book? Something that would make her life a little healthier and more enjoyable than it is now? What can she do about that?

Well, she can read through the last portion of my book, where I will include a collection of exercises, practices, and routines typical of those used in some of the therapies. Naturally, they will have to be limited to those Shelley can do by herself, without the aid and supervision of a therapist.

So—

If my friend Shelley can hold on just a bit longer, she should be able to find that missing puzzle piece and get a complete picture of herself.

I'd like nothing better! For her, for you, for everybody!

Part 1
Understanding Yourself

CHAPTER 1
ARE YOU READY TO GET BETTER?

You don't have to be sick to want to get better.

You may have a problem that keeps you from enjoying life. You may not like the way you behave in certain situations. You may have some anxieties and fears you'd like to get rid of. You may be tense and unable to relax. Even a little pressure may make you uncomfortable. Maybe you worry more than you think you should. Maybe you'd like to get more out of your sex life. Make friends more easily and keep them longer. Be a more creative person.

Perhaps you suspect that you have some potential you haven't been able to develop—or even discover. Perhaps your life could use a little more zest—or a lot more serenity. Or you feel lumpy, dumpy, old before your time. Maybe your needs aren't being fulfilled—or you don't know what your needs are.

In other words, you aren't getting satisfaction out of life. And you should be.

Ah-h-h-h!

Satisfaction is a great big *ah-h-h-h!* that comes from the mind, the body, the heart, and the spirit. It comes when we know who and what we are in the very deepest sense, and when we are making the most complete use of our total selves. Satisfaction comes from being the best and the most we can possibly be.

So if you are not getting satisfaction and you want to be the best you can be, then you have every right to want to get better—because getting better will bridge the distance between where you are and where you want to be.

Instead of asking yourself, "What's wrong with me?" ask yourself, "How can I have more satisfaction in my life?" and go on from there.

Why so many helping hands?

If you were a caveman or cavewoman, your life would be a lot simpler. I don't mean it would be happier, because prehistoric men and women had their hard times, too, but of a much different kind.

If you had to worry about such things as starvation, bitter cold, monstrous beasts, and hostile neighbors, you wouldn't have time to worry about anything else. Your energies would be outer-directed, in self-defense. You would know little or nothing about yourself, and you wouldn't care, because the most important thing in your life would be staying alive.

But you're not a caveman or cavewoman. You're a member of a progressive, highly developed society. You don't have to worry about marauding beasts and the bitter winds of winter. You eat well, dress well, live well, and you can look forward to living that way for a long, long time. Your energies, therefore, are more inner-directed. You not only explore your world, you explore yourself. In fact, there isn't any really new territory in the world today. It's all been charted and traveled. It's known, familiar. But that inner world, the world of the self—now there's an adventure! You can always find something new there. And no two inner worlds are the same.

Nor does that inner world remain as you find it. It changes. Constantly. It is very complex, and where you find complexity, you also find problems. One part of ourselves gets out of kilter, and all the other parts are affected.

So, because we are progressive and highly developed, and because we are complex, we have many different kinds of problems. The caveman had only physical, tangible hardships. Ours are physical, psychological, philosophical, emotional, spiritual, sexual, and social. That is why there are now so many different kinds of ways to get better.

It wouldn't make any sense to have only one solution for all kinds of human problems. There are too many different kinds of human beings and too many different kinds of problems. While it may be confusing to confront the many therapies available to us today, the variety is absolutely necessary. Somewhere there is a technique that is just right for each of us. The trick is to find it.

A point of view

Another reason why there are so many different kinds of help for our problems is that no two persons experience life in exactly the same way. Sigmund Freud had one point of view, B. F. Skinner another. Consequently, each man developed a different theory about why we have problems and what we can do to solve them.

Those who are comfortable with Freud's point of view say, "Hey, your problems began when you were a child. Something happened then to make you feel the way you do now. Go to a psychotherapist and tell her about your early life. Go way, way back—as far as you can—until you remember what happened. Then relive the experience and get a new perspective on it. Once you understand why you feel the way you do, you won't feel that way anymore."

"Nonsense!" say those who prefer the Skinner point of view. "Forget what happened so many years ago. That isn't important here and now. What you need is to learn how to behave in a new way. If you think something is blocking your way in life, don't try to remove it. We'll show you how to go around it."

Freud and Skinner, of course, are worlds apart in their

points of view, and in between are a growing number of other points of view. Some overlap, but each one is unique in some way. And each one began because someone wanted to help us get more out of our lives.

Some require more time than others, some cost more than others, some are more easily available in all parts of the country. Some have been around a long time, and some are very new.

Three ways to get better

If something isn't quite right with your life, there are three basic categories of help available: therapies, growth techniques, and body techniques.

Therapies are aimed at helping you solve your problems. If you're the kind of person who keeps putting obstacles in your own path—or if someone else has put them there—then one of the therapies should be able to help you remove them. If you're your own worst enemy, if you always seem to be the loser instead of the winner and you don't know why, try one of the therapies. What you need is a psychological survival kit, and this is where you can find one.

Growth techniques pick up where therapies leave off. If you feel okay most of the time, fine. Now, go on from there and discover your potential. You have abilities and strengths you didn't even know existed, and the growth techniques are designed to help you find out what they are. Want to overcome your shyness? Want to be able to relax in the midst of stress? Want to achieve higher states of concentration and consciousness? Try a growth technique.

Body techniques are based upon the conviction that mind and body are interrelated, and that the condition of one will eventually affect the condition of the other. Of course, we already know about such things as psychosomatic illnesses—physical illness caused by mental or emotional stress or trauma. But the relationship can work the other way around, too, and this is the area that body techniques attempt to emphasize. For instance, our psychological problems may cause us to stand or walk in a certain way, or perhaps to breathe with difficulty at certain times. Our heartbeat may accelerate unexpectedly and uncomfortably, or we may become nervous and tense. If we solve our psychological problems, that's wonderful. But what about the physical part of ourselves? Chances are we still walk the wrong way, or our heart beats too rapidly at times, or we're rigid with tension when we don't have any reason to be that way. If so, then one of the body techniques can help by making us aware of the way our bodies work and by teaching us to gain control of its functions—actually enabling us to undo the physical pain caused by psychological stress. Also, these techniques can help prevent the psychological pain that comes from a neglected and underdeveloped body.

Until recently, analytical psychotherapy was the only "accepted" and "scientifically oriented" way to get better. In the 1960s Eastern thought was gradually making its way into the Western world, but it was considered strictly for hippies. It was all right for the Beatles to hang around with gurus and talk about a higher level of consciousness, but not the man in the three-piece suit. A gentle-speaking, soft-eyed man named Maharishi Mahesh Yogi had just come to the United States hoping to teach us all—absolutely free—the art of transcendental meditation, but except for a few farsighted students there were no takers. In those days the only proper place to get better was the analyst's couch—and if that's where you went, you didn't tell everybody about it.

And then, when East and West began to meet, they found they could get along very well together.

Instead of offering transcendental meditation free, somebody got the bright idea of charging a fee and offering the information in a series of lessons. Perhaps, to our mass-marketing-influenced minds, this gave the technique more value ("You get what you pay for"). Or perhaps we Westerners appreciate something that exacts some form of sacrifice from us. Whatever the reason, TM caught on. Thousands and then hundreds of thousands of people tried it and had such praise for its stress-relieving methods that finally the Establishment had to stop fighting and start joining. Today TM is being taught in public schools, offered free of charge to employees by many businesses, and has reached others through millions of copies of books on the subject.

And that was only the beginning. Suddenly the floodgates were opened, and in poured an incredible number of different ways to correct whatever wasn't quite right in your life. And each one was greeted with an almost desperate eagerness, because so many people were hungry for the same thing—satisfaction. That great big *ah-h-h-h!*

Besides the traditional analytic form of therapy, we now have Primal Therapy, Gestalt therapy, group therapy, sex therapy, transactional therapy, assertiveness training, Silva Mind Control, Arica training, biofeedback, Rolfing, many types of yoga, megavitamin therapy, est, transcendental meditation, and many others too numerous to list. Some therapists are now combining several methods to achieve greater flexibility in meeting the individual needs of their patients. Therapy à la carte!

Inner ecology

As one man put it after completing a course in mind control, "We hear a lot of talk about the environment and how we ought to clean it up. But we all have an inner environment, too, and it's time we paid some attention to that. That's where everything's happening, anyway—on the inside!"

A West Coast artist put it this way: "My husband and I

had just about everything—or so we thought. We were successful in our work, we had a lovely house, our children were strong and healthy and apparently didn't have any major problems. But then, one day Bill and I looked at each other and wondered if it was just like the song says—'Is that all there is?' Were we going to continue paying our bills and putting some money away and adding more things to our lives—until someday we would die?

"Now I'm glad we came to that point, because it was the beginning of a whole new kind of existence. For us, Hatha yoga and meditation made the difference. We're not just an accumulation of things anymore—we're more loving, more understanding of ourselves and each other. We're far more creative."

"I had reached the top," an executive of a large corporation says, "but I wanted something more. The amazing thing is, I found it inside myself." He is in group therapy.

"I thought I was going to spend the rest of my life in the same old job, at the same old salary," said a woman who recently moved up into the managerial level of her company. "I blamed other people for the rut I was in." Then she accompanied a friend to a lecture about assertiveness training and realized she was exactly the kind of person who needed the course. She signed up. "I had no one to blame but myself," she says now. "I wasn't able to speak up and ask for something I deserved. Well, now I can, and it makes all the difference in the world. I feel so much better about everybody now."

These comments are typical of those who are finding satisfaction in growth techniques.

But what of the others? If there are so many of us who crave satisfaction, then there must be a great deal of *dis*satisfaction in our society. Right you are!

We are dissatisfied because we aren't fulfilled. We're taking what life gives us instead of shaping our lives to suit our unique needs. There are parts of ourselves we aren't even using, haven't even discovered. We aren't productive enough, creative enough, loving enough. There is so much we still don't know—about ourselves, about others, about the universe. We are more than material beings. We have feelings, thoughts, a spirit—what are we doing about them?

We are dissatisfied because we are beginning to realize that happiness doesn't come from outside ourselves. It comes from the inside—from that "inner environment" we have ignored for so long as we scrambled about, trying to accumulate the things that were supposed to make us happy, but didn't. And couldn't.

Real happiness comes when our inner ecology is properly balanced, when we have the satisfied feeling that all the many different parts of ourselves are working smoothly.

And now, for the first time ever, each one of us has the opportunity to achieve that balanced inner ecology. The tools, the knowledge, the information, the training are there for us to choose.

You don't have to be sick to want to get better. You just have to be dissatisfied—and want satisfaction!

Choose your own lifestyle

Recently I had a visit from a young woman I hadn't seen for a long time. The change in her was remarkable, almost unbelievable, and absolutely wonderful.

I could barely remember the way she used to slouch in her chair when she came to my office. Her voice was so wispy I had difficulty hearing her. She was so utterly defeated, it was hard for me to be objective about her plight and to keep from throwing my arms around her to comfort her.

Leslie's husband had walked out on her, leaving her with the total care of their two small children. Understandably, she was crushed, almost leveled. She kept defending herself, explaining that she had been a good wife and mother, had been a great cook and housekeeper, thrifty with money, and always solicitous of her husband's career. And then he went off with another woman. Why? she kept asking herself.

It was very hard to get Leslie's mind on the present, much less the future, but gradually—and painfully—she began to accept the reality of her situation. Whatever had happened in the past was beyond her control, but the present—and the future—were something else. They had to be created from scratch. And quickly.

The last time I had seen Leslie she was going into group therapy guided by a most skillful psychiatrist. She was nervous about mingling with other women and men who, she was certain, were in much better psychological shape than she was. But that was a perfectly natural reaction, as I was able to assure her.

The group experience did wonders for Leslie. Through her relationships with the other members, she was able to evaluate herself as a person rather than as a reject. Little by little she gained insight into who she really was and where she wanted to go.

Well—here she was, a vibrant, beautiful young woman who sat up straight and looked me right in the eye as she spoke in a perfectly clear and musical voice. She was full of self-confidence and *joie de vivre.*

"Remember how nervous I was about meeting all those other people?" she said. "What a dummy I was! I thought *I* had problems! But when I found out what was happening in other people's lives, I saw that I was pretty lucky.

"And then, the biggest discovery of all was that I could become anything I wanted to be. I didn't have to repeat my past life. I could choose a whole new lifestyle! I could have control over what I do, what I feel—everything!"

With that discovery, Leslie had gone out and gotten a job. Then she began taking design courses at night so that eventually she could get a better job in a field she found stimulating but had never dared think she could enter. Her mother helped care for her two children.

Leslie also had lost weight, which was good, and she wore the kind of clothes that did things for her. I wasn't surprised to learn that there was a man in her life. "But nothing serious," she said. "I want to finish discovering myself, and then I'll think about discovering someone else."

Here was a woman who was choosing her own present and future. The group experience helped her opt for *satisfaction.*

You don't need a trauma like Leslie's to make you aware of the choices in your life. In fact, thanks to the attention given them by the media, you are surrounded by them. Perhaps overwhelmed by them. Every time you open a newspaper or a magazine you read about some new form of therapy, some new level of consciousness to explore, some previously unrealized spiritual world that can be yours, a method of regulating bodily processes that were thought to be uncontrollable. Each new technique is fascinating, but before you can learn more about one, you open another magazine or turn on your TV and find another, newer, more marvelous procedure. How can you possibly keep up with them?

You can't. There aren't that many hours in a day or years in a lifetime. So the next best thing is to concentrate on whichever therapy or technique is right for *you.* And that's what this book will enable you to do.

In the next several chapters you will be able to find out what it is like to experience the most widely accepted new and not-so-new therapies, growth techniques, and body techniques. You'll learn how they work, and how much of your time they require.

Then the choice is up to you. You can expand your horizons, your consciousness, your supply of energy, your spiritual domain. Whatever you like.

Ah-h-h-h!

CHAPTER 2
THERAPIES

Joan is uncomfortable whenever she feels angry. Sometimes she tries so hard to hold her temper that she has difficulty breathing. In fact, she tries to be the most agreeable person on earth just to avoid confrontations. But the more agreeably she behaves, the angrier she feels.

Hal has a hard time relating to women. He was engaged once, but broke it off at the last moment because—well, he really doesn't know why. Somehow the thought of getting married scared him. Actually, he'd like to have a home of his own. He doesn't like living with his aging mother, and he keeps saying he's going to move out and get his own apartment. But he never does. The last woman he went out with was a very lovely person, and Hal enjoyed every minute he spent with her. Then he started getting serious, and that's when it happened. Hal provoked an argument, which gave him an excuse to overreact and break off the relationship. Now Hal's worried about ever being able to have a relationship.

Sybil works too hard. She's aware of it, but can't seem to do anything about it. Even though she's a good administrator, she's always afraid of getting fired. She never takes a vacation, because she's afraid the company will learn to do without her. She starts her day an hour earlier than anyone else, and works long after others have gone home. She keeps finding fault with herself and does her work over and over, trying to be perfect and never succeeding. She really wishes she could relax and enjoy her work, but she can't. The more praise she gets, the more anxious she becomes. Are they saying those nice things because they really want to ease her out of the picture?

Lee is ambitious. He'd like to become president of the company someday and run it his way. But getting to the top means doing some things that go against the grain. Worst of all, it means allowing his job to become the only important thing in his life. He works a seven-day, seven-evening week and rarely takes a vacation—not because his work load is so heavy, but because he's trying to demonstrate to the people in power his dedication. He doesn't want to spend all his time working. He enjoys the company of his wife and children. He doesn't want to get involved in the power plays going on around him, but if he doesn't, he might be their victim. Sometimes he thinks he'd like to chuck it all and open a fishing camp up in Maine. Of course, that's just a fantasy. He's got to get to the top, although he really couldn't tell you why. It's just something that keeps pushing him.

The people described above have problems they can't solve because they don't know what the problems are and they aren't in touch with themselves. Something deep inside them, possibly something that happened when they were young, keeps tripping them up. They do things they don't really want to do, and very often they can't fulfill their real desires. Often they don't know what their real desires are. Consequently, they often feel so frustrated that they cease to be productive and creative. They may become so preoccupied with avoiding the experience of failure that they do indeed continue to fail. They aren't what you would call sick, but they certainly would like to feel better about themselves.

Here is where therapy comes in, because therapy aims to help a person solve his problems by enabling him to understand who he is and why he behaves as he does. Some people say a therapy is problem-oriented, but I prefer to think of it as problem-*solving*-oriented.

Most therapies are verbal experiences in which the patient

and the therapist (or, in the case of group therapy, the patient group and the therapist) discuss the patient's feelings on increasingly deeper levels of her being. Some therapies also include physical expressions of the patient's inner feelings. In almost all therapies the therapist and the therapist's personality is of great importance to the procedure.

So in a therapy you might expect to talk, listen, laugh, cry, scream, lie on a couch, sit in a chair, touch strangers, touch someone you know very well, pound your fist into a mat, become enraged, relax, daydream, fantasize, and tell the absolute truth as you never have known it before. It all depends upon the therapy you choose.

Whichever one it is, a therapy can help you restore your control over what now seem out-of-control areas of your life. It can enable you to overcome the problems that might otherwise do you in.

CHAPTER 3 BEHAVIOR THERAPY

Recently I was watching a dog trainer work with a six-month-old puppy. The trainer and the dog obviously had a very good rapport. Each trusted the other. For a while the trainer allowed the dog to amble along with him, sometimes close to his heels, sometimes at a distance, and sometimes going off in an entirely different direction. The puppy was wearing a collar with a lead attached but left trailing.

Then the trainer took the end of the lead in his hand and the lesson began. As the trainer took a step forward, the puppy scampered off in another direction, only to be stopped by the taut lead. Stubbornly, the puppy sat down. The trainer stopped, reached down, and patted the puppy's head. "Heel!" the trainer said enthusiastically, as if they both were going to have a marvelous time. The puppy started forward, then stopped and sat down again.

This time the trainer stopped and looked at the dog sternly. "No!" he said, firmly but not angrily.

The trainer took his position next to the puppy and said, "Heel!" again in the same let's-have-a-ball tone of voice. Now the puppy took a few steps alongside the trainer.

"Good dog!" said the trainer, reaching down to pat the dog's shoulder as he spoke. "Heel!"

The puppy seemed rather proud of itself and marched along. Then it stopped and sat down again, sullenly.

The trainer was amazingly patient. He repeated what he had done before. He said "No!" in a scolding voice and returned to the dog's right side. Then he said "Heel!" and off they went.

These routines were repeated for about fifteen minutes, and each time the puppy walked along a little farther at the trainer's side. Once it refused to heel at all, but the trainer said "Good dog!" and that did it. The puppy bounded along, heeling quite well, and seemed to have forgotten about sitting down. Its tail wagged vigorously each time the trainer said "Good dog!" and reached down to pat it.

When the lesson was over I complimented the trainer on his work, and he said something interesting.

"Well, you just have to realize that the dog wants to take the easy way out—same as people do. So you have to make the right way the easy way."

What a very good insight into behavior therapy!

Green means go

When the traffic light turns red, you put your foot on the brake, don't you? When the light turns green, your foot goes to the accelerator, right?

Stand next to a telephone pole and what happens? Nothing. But stand next to an attractive person and you begin to feel excited.

When the boss walks into the room, you try to look busy. The moment she leaves, you can relax and have a good laugh over a joke your associate just told you.

Maybe you don't like to look out the window on the sixtieth floor, because you feel as if you're going to fall out. Or is it planes that scare you?

The reason for these reactions is that in each case you have learned to behave in a particular way. Something in the environment acts as a *stimulus* and you respond to it in the way you have been taught, just as the puppy was taught, to respond.

Of course you stop for a red light. You were taught to do that when you learned to drive, and you know that if you don't stop you'll get a ticket. Green means you can go ahead, which is a very pleasant feeling you have no reason to avoid.

You don't want to incur the boss's displeasure because it produces very uncomfortable feelings in you, so you look busy when she's around. When she's gone, you can have a good time.

As for the telephone pole and the attractive person—well, you were simply reacting, or responding, to the stimulus, which is what you do all the time, even if you aren't aware of it. In the case of the sixtieth-floor window or the plane, you were reacting to an unpleasant stimulus in your past.

The condition is what counts

When you keep reacting in the same way to the same stimulus, your response becomes *conditioned*. You don't even think about what you are doing or whether you have any choice in the matter. You simply associate a certain response with a certain stimulus, and that's that. You may not even remember or know why. You just do it.

If your response to the stimulus is the right one, you have no reason to be upset about it, and in fact you should feel comfortable about it. You repeat the response any time the stimulus is present and you get the response you want. And that is called *positive reinforcement*. Each time you respond in the right way you feel better about it, until finally it becomes second nature.

Remember the first time you ever entered a library? Probably, as soon as you walked in someone said "Sh-h-h!" and put a finger to his lips. You also saw cards and posters bearing the word SILENCE. Everyone else was walking around on tiptoe and speaking in whispers. So you obeyed the command and were quiet. You tiptoed and whispered, and everyone smiled approval. And you felt good about yourself. So each time you went to the library you were quiet and found approval. Now, whenever you enter a room lined with books you immediately begin to whisper and tiptoe—without even thinking about it.

But if you respond in the wrong way to a stimulus, your behavior may bring on feelings of anxiety and fear, which is something you certainly won't want to repeat. For example, if you're not supposed to make personal calls at work and you get caught doing it, the reprimand you get from your boss will make you very uncomfortable. Maybe you think it's a silly rule and you feel you have every right to contact a friend during the day so long as you get your work done, but the next time you reach for the phone to make a personal call, you'll feel that same discomfort. Perhaps even more. Finally you'll stop calling your friends, because it's more comfortable to obey the rules, however you may gripe about them.

What you just experienced is called *negative reinforcement.* You responded in the wrong way to the presence of the telephone and you got punished by way of a reprimand. That made you feel anxious, queasy, perhaps afraid. The next time you reached for the phone to make a personal call, the punishment-related feelings reoccurred, so you stopped. And when you stopped, the bad feelings also stopped—at which point you were experiencing negative reinforcement.

Eventually, through positive and negative reinforcement, you become conditioned to respond in the most comfortable, least-anxiety-producing way—which means that the right way is now the easy way.

Albert and the white rat

Up to now we've been discussing simple forms of conditioning. But stimulus doesn't always come to us in simple ways, and when it gets complicated, that's when we can run into trouble.

Once upon a time, back in 1920, two behaviorists conducted a study using a baby named Albert and a white rat (who shall remain nameless). When Albert first saw the white rat, he had no fear of it. When the rat was placed near him, Albert reached out to stroke its soft white fur. This was allowed to happen several times.

Then, as Albert reached out toward the white rat, he heard a loud unpleasant noise quite close to him (*aversion stimulus*, or punishment), and he pulled back his hand. He reached out again, and the same thing happened. Albert began to cry. When the rat was removed, the noise ceased, and Albert stopped crying (negative reinforcement). Then, when the rat was placed near Albert, he began to cry at the sight of the rat, even though this time there was no accompanying unpleasant sound. Albert had been conditioned to associate the sound with the sight of the rat, and to avoid hearing the sound (and thereby feeling anxious). Albert simply didn't want to see the rat at all.

The study continued. A white rabbit was placed near Albert. Albert had never expressed any fear of a rabbit before, but suddenly he began to cry, and kept crying until the rabbit was removed. Next, Albert was presented with a white furry glove and then a ball of cotton, and each time he cried. His conditioned response of fear had become *generalized*, which means he associated a feeling of fear with anything soft and white.

Albert was part of a controlled study. The stimulus in his environment was limited to whatever the experimenters chose to place there. No so with life.

Our environment is chock full of stimuli, and sometimes our responses get mixed up.

For instance:

You're walking along the street and you come to a busy intersection which you must cross to continue on your way. Cars are whizzing past and heavy trucks make the ground beneath your feet vibrate ominously. You notice that the traffic light remains green for only a few seconds, which means that you must cross the street quickly.

For a moment you respond to the noises of the traffic. You experience some fear. That's fine, because you ought to be a bit afraid in a situation like this, and your response to fear will be caution. You wait until the light turns back to red, then to green, and again to red as you estimate how fast you will have to walk to cross safely. When the light turns green again, you respond to it by walking quickly—and safely—to the other side and go on your way.

But suppose you came to the busy intersection and stood rooted to the sidewalk, responding to the traffic noises with paralyzing fear. You see the light turn green, then red, then green and red over and over again. Suddenly, you turn and run. You are responding to the light as you would to the traffic noises. You are running from the fear the noises made you feel, and now you associate anxiety and fear with a green light. Your response is mixed up—you're just like Albert and his white rat.

You run all the way home and slam the door behind you. Now you feel safe. You don't see any traffic lights and you can't hear those big wheels spinning and whizzing past you. But you don't want to go outside again, ever. You'll stay home, for good.

Albert may have been able to get through life without cuddling up to a white rat, a rabbit, a glove, or a ball of cotton. But you can't very well remain a productive human being and stay locked behind closed doors all your life. You've got a problem.

What a therapist will tell you

A behaviorist is more interested in what you do than in what you feel. Not that your feelings aren't of some importance. Of course they are. If you can't cross a street because you're afraid, then your fear is very important. But a behaviorist would say that it isn't your response to the stimulus (fear) that keeps you from crossing, but rather the stimulus itself—

the heavy traffic—that you should concern yourself with.

Let me explain:

You learned to respond to the fear stimulus—and what you learned, you can unlearn. If your responses were conditioned by repetition, or even if they have become generalized, they can be *deconditioned*. And in their place you can learn new, more appropriate responses—which means that, yes, you can be trained to cross a street filled with traffic that scares you half to death. You can learn to respond, not to the traffic noise but to the green light that says go. In other words, you can learn *not* to respond to the fear-causing stimulus and instead respond to a different stimulus.

Systematic desensitization

For example, let's take the case of a young pianist who was about to make his concert debut.

For years Julian had played beautifully, but only alone or in the presence of his teacher and family. Although the thought of performing before a large audience made him uneasy, he assumed that was quite normal. And so it was.

But a few moments before Julian was to go onstage he began to sweat profusely. His hands felt cold, almost numb. He walked onstage, took his seat at the piano, and swallowed hard. His mouth was bone-dry. His arms felt like lead. He knew he could not even touch the keys, and any attempt at a performance was out of the question. Terrified and embarrassed, Julian stood up, looked out at the audience helplessly, and walked off into the wings.

Immediately Julian sought help, and he decided to see a behavior therapist. During their first meeting the therapist asked Julian to describe his problem and to give him a complete history of any other occasions during which he had responded with the same kind of anxiety. As Julian spoke, he had the feeling that the therapist was an understanding person and not in the least judgmental. He could trust the therapist.

Then the therapist told Julian he was confident they could solve the problem, and he even described exactly how they would do it.

The therapist explained that it was impossible for a person to be both relaxed and anxious at the same time. Since performing before a large audience made Julian anxious, he would be retrained to learn how to relax at the thought of performing. Once he responded to performing with a feeling of relaxation, he could not possibly become anxious.

Of course, it would take time. Anywhere from a few months to half a year. And the therapist would need Julian's complete cooperation. Julian agreed, and the program of *systematic desensitization* began.

The first thing Julian had to learn to do was relax deeply and in response to his own desire. As Julian lay on a couch the therapist asked him to imagine a lovely, peaceful scene, perhaps a special place that he had enjoyed at some time in his life. As Julian began to construct the scene in his mind, he felt his body easing into a more comfortable position. Then the therapist told him to begin tensing and relaxing various muscles—in his hands, his forearms, his upper arms, his shoulders, his neck.

"Clench your fists," the therapist would say. "Now relax them. See what a difference that makes?"

Julian was amazed. He had had no idea how deeply he could teach his body to relax.

This procedure went on for several visits, and it took Julian about two months to master the art of relaxation so completely that he could untense his entire body at will. He also practiced at home with the aid of a cassette of instructions the therapist had given him.

Now Julian and his therapist began to work on a list of

performance-related situations that provoked Julian's anxiety. They came up with eight kinds of stimuli, arranged in order from the least anxiety-producing to the most:

1. Julian playing alone.
2. Julian playing with only his teacher in the room.
3. Julian playing while a stranger stands outside the room.
4. Julian playing while a stranger is in the room.
5. Julian playing in a large but empty concert hall.
6. Julian performing on the stage, but with only his family and a few friends as an audience.
7. Julian performing before an audience of strangers.
8. Julian performing before an audience of professional musicians.

Bravo! Bravo!

Finally, the list and the art of relaxation were brought together.

"Relax," the therapist said, "and imagine yourself in the first situation. You are playing the piano by yourself. No one else is in the room. No one else can hear you."

Julian felt himself unwind at the thought of this assignment. He had no difficulty imagining himself playing alone. He remained completely relaxed. His therapist asked him to repeat this process several times, and each time Julian did it with ease.

Then, during the next session, the therapist went on to situation 2: "Imagine yourself playing the piano, and imagine your teacher in the room with you."

At first Julian remained relaxed. Then he began to feel anxious and his body tensed.

"Stop!" the therapist said, noting Julian's taut muscles. "You must regain a state of relaxation. Now go back to that beautiful mountain scene you love so much. Lie on the grass and listen to the leaves move in the breeze. Relax."

Julian was frustrated and impatient, but he followed the therapist's instructions. It was difficult to reconstruct the peaceful scene he loved, but he kept trying, and finally he could actually see the mountains around him and feel the fresh breeze against his face. Slowly Julian regained his feeling of comfort—and with it a sense of triumph. Soon he could imagine himself playing a most difficult piece while his teacher stood at the piano beside him—and Julian remained relaxed. Not a trace of anxiety.

What happened to Julian happened many times throughout his therapy. As he reached out toward more tension-producing situations, he lost his feeling of relaxation, and once that happened, anxiety rushed in. But his therapist took him back to an earlier stage of development where Julian could regain his feeling of ease, and proceed again from there. This is known as *corrective reinforcement.*

Within a few more months Julian and his therapist were able to go through the entire list of anxiety-provoking situations—with Julian completely relaxed. The very thought of performing, even in the presence of professional musicians, now provoked the response of relaxation.

Basically the therapy was completed at this point, although the therapist also attended Julian's first concert—at which, I might add, Julian's performance received excellent reviews.

Where BT works best

If you have phobias and anxieties—such as fear of flying—behavior therapy can help you. If you want to get rid of some habits that handicap your well-being and productiveness—smoking, overeating, etc.—look into BT.

Some critics of behavior modification techniques say that they do not go deep enough or get to the root cause of a problem. Proponents of BT feel, however, that in most traditional forms of psychotherapy too much time is spent on root causes and not enough on solutions to problems.

Without a doubt, BT is a much shorter process than analytical psychotherapy. The cost per therapy hour is about the same—ranging from thirty-five to seventy-five dollars—but the duration of therapy is only a matter of months, compared to years.

CHAPTER 4
GESTALT THERAPY

I do my thing, and you do your thing.
I am not in this world to live up to your expectations.
And you are not in this world to live up to mine.
You are you, and I am I,
And if by chance we find each other, it's beautiful.
If not, it can't be helped.

This is the Gestalt Prayer. It was written by Fritz Perls, the originator of Gestalt therapy, and it pretty much summarizes what the therapy is and is not.

Gestalt therapy does not attempt to solve what you think is your problem. It does not aim to help you understand *why* you behave as you do. It will not urge you to change or try to become another kind of person.

It *will* help you to become *aware*—of yourself, of others, of your environment.

Don't talk to a Gestalt therapist about your past. He isn't interested. Don't speculate about the future. That doesn't exist.

What does exist, and what interests the therapist immensely, is you, here and now. He wants to know what you are feeling and thinking this very moment, because those thoughts and feelings influence your awareness of reality. And if you are not truly aware, then that is your problem.

The growling stomach

Suppose you just sat down at your desk to balance your checkbook. You'd like to get that little chore out of the way before you have lunch and go on to other things.

At first you concentrate on your checkbook and you're aware of very little else. But gradually, as you punch out the figures on your pocket calculator, you realize that you are getting hungry. You try to work faster, but, maddeningly, your mind begins to wander. You remember what a good dinner you had last evening. The steak was perfect, the coffee delicious. You can almost smell them now.

Back to your checkbook!

Then you find yourself lingering over a canceled check you cashed at the supermarket last week. That reminds you—you need a box of cereal. And a can of tomatoes. You wonder if asparagus is in season yet.

The checkbook! Of course.

You're almost finished when your stomach begins to growl. Suddenly it doesn't seem so important to balance your checkbook before lunch. Why not finish after lunch?

Good idea. Let's eat!

A short time later you return to your desk. You notice the sun coming through the window to your right. It's a lovely day. The children are out in the street playing stickball, and the happy sound of their voices is most pleasant. You feel the sun on your shoulder as you work. How nice that is! You get right down to work, and in no time you're finished. Good.

What you need is what you see

Why couldn't you keep your mind on your checkbook when you began to work on it?

Because you weren't aware of it.

And why, after you had lunch, did you see and hear things you hadn't noticed before—the sunshine, the lovely day, the children playing?

Because you *were* aware of them.

What made the difference? Your needs.

When you first sat down at your desk your need was to balance your checkbook. You were aware of it and could concentrate. But quite soon that need was pushed into the background by a more urgent need—you were hungry and wanted to eat. Thoughts related to food came into your awareness, blocking out other things. Between your need to work and your need to eat, you didn't even notice what kind of day it was. You didn't see the sun or hear the children playing, although they were there at the time. You weren't aware of them then because your needs weren't related to them.

After you satisfied your hunger, your need to work on your checkbook wasn't urgent enough to block out the other sights and sounds around you. You were then able to "make contact" with more parts of your immediate environment. You were aware of your feelings, your thoughts, and your reality of that moment. *Gestalt*—which means *a meaningful organized wholeness*—had taken place. Once this happens, you can choose which parts of yourself you want to satisfy at the moment. For instance, in this example the checkbook can wait until later, because it is more important to hear, see, and sense your environment.

Don't tell me why

In Gestalt therapy, the patient attempts to become more aware of his own needs so that he can realize how those needs influence his perception of reality. He doesn't delve into how his needs arose, because that would lead him to analyze, to intellectualize about them. No—instead he seeks to experience his needs, to feel them and bring them out into the open so that he can say, *Yes, I see you, and you are part of me. I may not like you or I may absolutely adore you, but that doesn't matter. What I feel is part of me. Everything I feel is part of me.*

Gestaltists believe it is natural for all parts of the human being to come together. It is unnatural, or neurotic, for any of them to be rejected by the self. And if any of them are rejected, then they cannot play their proper part in influencing our awareness of reality.

For instance, to understand our environment intellectually is not enough. Neither is it enough to respond only through emotion to what is going on around us and inside us. In either instance, we are not responding with a complete perception of what is going on. We are satisfying only certain needs, to the exclusion of others—which is what a Gestaltist would call *irresponsible behavior.*

Responsible behavior occurs only when the person is aware of his needs, even the conflicting ones, and can choose the kind of behavior that will nurture them.

The act of choosing is called *creative adjustment.*

But how?

Okay.

Somewhere along the way in your life, your needs became fragmented. Some of them you accepted and some you rejected, and now you don't even know which are which. Perhaps, like Lee in Chapter 2, you played up your mental abilities at the expense of your feelings, and now you "can't feel." So what do you do?

You invite all your needs to come out into the open, to make their demands on you and put you in touch with those things in your environment that are meaningful to them.

But how? That is the question you will be asking yourself in Gestalt therapy. Not *why*, but *how?*

You can work solely with your therapist or in a group directed by the therapist. More often you'll work in a group, because you will need the members' support and encouragement as you seek to express who and what you really are.

Although the therapeutic techniques vary with the therapists, the most popular one is called the *empty chair*. And it is just that—an empty chair placed opposite the patient, who sits on another chair. Then the patient begins to tell the therapist (and the group) what she is feeling at that very moment. Never mind what she felt yesterday or any other day. Forget about how she wants to feel tomorrow. *Now*. Only *now* counts.

Suppose the patient is a man who has come into therapy because he is disturbed about his sexual performance. He has premature ejaculations.

Instead of discussing the possible causes of these premature ejaculations, the patient will be encouraged (by the therapist and the group) to express his present feelings about his sexual needs. Fairly quickly he will begin to reveal that part of himself which feels he should be an excellent lover each and every time he has intercourse. This rather bossy part of himself is called the *overdog*. But then the therapist will tell the patient to sit in the empty chair and answer these overdog demands. Enter the *underdog*, a more submissive yet stubborn part of the same person that poutingly pits itself against the wishes of the overdog. Overdog says, *Be a great lover!* and underdog answers, *But I'm afraid I'll be a lousy lover*.

Back and forth, from one chair to the other, the patient moves, not arguing with himself, but allowing his conflicting needs to argue with each other. And in so doing, he is bringing those needs out into the open in the presence of a group that constantly reassures him that it is all right for him to do this.

Perhaps the patient was not aware of his conflicting needs. Perhaps he had shut one of them out because he felt it was unacceptable. But in doing that, he closed off a part of his awareness of life and was therefore not free to choose the kind of behavior that would be most satisfying to him.

As the dialogue continues, the patient begins to see that both overdog and underdog are parts of him, and that if he excludes either one of them he cannot be whole. What if he doesn't like one part or the other? That doesn't matter. "You are you, and I am I," as the Prayer goes. He isn't here to please one or the other. He simply is here. And the choice of satisfying one need or the other is up to him.

Once a patient actually talks—argues—with a need, he becomes aware of it, which is the goal of Gestalt therapy. When one is aware of a need one can integrate it back into his being. In other words, he takes back into himself that which he once cast out. Gestalt—he is whole.

The empty chair also is very effective when a patient imagines himself talking with another person, especially one upon whom he projects all kinds of blame for the problems in his life. I once tried this technique with a friend who seemed to have a great deal of difficulty expressing his emotions. He didn't come to me for consultation. In fact, we had just finished playing a few sets of tennis and were having a cool drink in the shade of my porch.

Hank was one of those driven young men who seem to leap up the success ladder three rungs at a time. He was charming but distant, and even though he and I had known each other for years, he never would let his hair down.

Until that hot summer afternoon . . .

It wasn't that Hank told me what was bothering him. I don't think he knew. He just said he had been feeling very tense lately, and asked if there was anything he could do to unwind.

Off the top of my head?—no, there wasn't. Still, it was obvious from Hank's rigid posture, the set of his mouth, and the anxiety in his eyes that something inside him was at war with something else.

I led him to talk about himself, which he didn't like to do, but when I asked him about other members of his family, his voice became bitter, especially when he mentioned his mother.

"Imagine your mother is sitting in this empty chair," I said, pushing a comfortable big lounge chair around to face Hank.

Hank obviously thought I was a little strange, but he went along with the suggestion. When I told him to tell his mother how he felt about her, he was a little awkward at first. Then a little polite. And then it all came out.

A part of Hank deeply resented what he felt was his mother's lack of attention to him when he was a little boy. "No matter how well I did in school, you never praised me!" he said. "I never was good enough for you!"

"Hank, sit in the other chair now," I interrupted. "Be your mother and answer your accusations."

Hank had been sitting on the edge of his chair, but when he moved to the other chair he settled back into it.

"Well, Hank," said Hank as his mother, "you were too young to understand what a hard time I was having. Your father had died, and there I was, still a young woman, with three small children to bring up.

"I know I didn't fuss over you as much as I did your brother and sister—but, Hank, you just didn't need as much fussing. Even as a child, you were always able to take care of yourself. Since I had to spread my attention pretty thin in those days, I gave it where it was needed most—and you didn't need it as much as the others. But I always was proud of you. I thought you knew that."

Back and forth Hank went in a dialogue that was absolutely fascinating. Eventually he began to see that the feelings he was expressing as himself and as his mother—all of them—were actually his. Part of him wanted praise and the other part didn't think he should get it. Part of him wanted love from his mother, and part of him was angry at her. The struggle between the two parts caused a lot of tension—especially in a young man who was constantly achieving things, and also especially when one of those parts was neither acknowledged, accepted, nor satisfied by himself.

I wouldn't say that Hank is "cured" or has "solved his problem" or has "become a different person" since he was able to face his conflicting needs. But he certainly seems more relaxed, and I feel as if I know him better. He expresses his feelings more spontaneously than he ever did. When he wants attention he lets you know it—and since he is able to satisfy his own need for attention, he can also give it to others. I'd say that's a creative adjustment.

How long?

Unlike other forms of therapy, Gestalt therapy is not a matter of weekly sessions. Groups are formed and brought together for concentrated periods of time, such as weekends, with sometimes a few weeks between meetings. Therapy lasts about three or four months, and costs range from fifteen to twenty-five dollars per meeting.

A word about the makeup of the groups: The purpose of the group is to encourage the patient to express innermost feelings without fear of criticism, ridicule, or any other negative reaction. How the members of the group relate to one another is not important and is not considered a part of the therapy.

Who?

Since Gestalt therapy aims at freeing up the emotions, it is particularly helpful to people who tend to overintellectualize their experiences. If you are uncomfortable in close relationships or when you are in a group, if your feelings seem to be all bottled up, if you are plagued by guilt and resentment, then you may want to look into GT.

CHAPTER 5 GROUP THERAPY

The word *group* immediately arouses strong feelings: curiosity, partisanship, hostility. Of all the therapies, group is perhaps the most talked about and least understood.

Because . . .

Group has become a label for several entirely different, often contradictory, kinds of therapeutic techniques. Some are more traditional than others. Some are more widely accepted by established associations. And some embody methods that to many people seem just plain freaky.

The reason for group therapy is that in individual therapy a person can go just so far and no further in solving his relationship problems. He is, in a sense, working in a vacuum along with his therapist and has very little opportunity to try out in real situations the insights he has gained into his personal difficulties. True, he can leave his individual session and return to his family or working environment, but they are not controlled situations. Who knows what will happen when it becomes obvious that the person is undergoing changes in his personality and behavior which, in turn, will draw forth changed reactions to him? He may bite off more than he can chew, which may set him back in his individual therapy. Not that such setbacks can't be overcome in therapy —they usually are—but they take a lot of time and cause much anxiety.

In a group you get feedback from the other members about the way you are behaving. You cannot hide in a corner as easily as you might in your everyday life.

Group therapy gives a person an opportunity to explore

himself and attempt to understand his problems while at the same time maintaining a relationship with other persons—and in a controlled situation. The controlling agent is the presence of the therapist, or therapists, who can provoke or limit the interactions of the group members. The amount of control and the methods of controlling interactions vary as much as the types of groups themselves.

So when we use the word *group*, we may mean one of many things, and it is important to distinguish between the various types of group therapies. Even the structure of groups is different. For instance, in group psychotherapy the members are chosen by the therapist to *represent* basic family members who react to each other much as each one did in his original family. Peer groups, such as Alcoholics Anonymous and Overeaters Anonymous, offer support and encouragement as they attempt to solve a specific problem common to them all. Encounter group members challenge each other in an attempt to break down resistance to intimate relationships, and they are more concerned with facilitating emotional expression than the causes for its repression. Family therapists work with the actual family, rather than a representation of it, and their goal is to enable each individual family member to become aware of his subconscious attitudes toward the others. Nude marathon puts a person in touch with his innermost emotions, and the presence of other members is supportive and nurturing.

There are many other versions of group therapy, far too many to include here. For our purposes, only the most widely used groups will be discussed, but I think they are quite typical of the many different methods available.

GROUP PSYCHOTHERAPY

Traditional psychotherapeutic techniques can be used in a group as well as in individual sessions. The aim of the psychotherapy group is to solve the problems that began in a person's earlier stages of life and are now lodged in his unconscious. In some groups, such as marriage groups, the members may have similar problems—for instance, marital discord—but the origin of the problems will be as different as the backgrounds of each member. In most groups, however, the problems of the members are different and highly individual.

Suppose you took over your father's business when he died and you feel trapped in a job you wouldn't ordinarily have chosen for yourself. But you don't want to sell the business, because your mother begs you to remember all your father had put into it, and all of it just for you. You hate what you're doing, but you feel guilty about not appreciating what was handed to you on a silver platter. Worst of all, you have contempt for yourself and you're convinced that everyone else feels the same way about you. Consequently, you can't run the business well, you can't get along with people, and you're taking out your frustrations on your spouse and children.

Perhaps you have been seeing a psychotherapist for some time on an individual basis, and now she says she thinks you would benefit from joining one of her groups. She may continue to see you privately, although less frequently, while you work with the group once or twice a week, or you may work strictly with the group. Still another possibility is that you may go right into a group without any private sessions with the therapist. A lot depends upon the therapist's evaluation of the nature of your problem and the degree to which it handicaps you.

I want to be one of you

The group has just formed and this is your first meeting. There are ten of you when everyone is present, which is about the maximum size for effective group work. Obviously you have one thing in common: Your problem is handicapping your life.

The therapist asks each one of you to introduce yourself and tell the group a little about yourself, your background, and your problem. That's when you begin to see that, except for your unhappiness, you all have very little in common. Your ages range from twenty-two to fifty-seven. Two of you are professionals: one a lawyer, the other a pharmacist, both women. Among the other four men and four women are a bus driver, an electrician, a librarian, a department store clerk, and a secretary. Some of you seem to speak with ease, and some are awkward. One seems so quiet, you wonder whether she has a voice at all.

The diversity of the group is intentional, and it took the therapist some time to organize ten people whose characteristics and problems would present challenges to each other.

You haven't been much of a talker yet. You're too busy listening. Finally you realize that you are comparing yourself with the others. And things don't look too good. First of all, you know you could never reveal certain things about yourself to the others. They'd throw you out if they knew what you really were like. And you wonder if you really belong in this group at all. You don't want to leave—not so far, anyway—but you're a little worried that they may ask you to go.

Just then, Joan, by far the most compulsive person in the group, announces that she came across a "perfectly wonderful article on neurosis" in some magazine and she'd like to bring it in to the group's next meeting. *Why does she want to do that?* you wonder. *Does she want to wallow in being neurotic?*

Well, here's what has been happening...

Beneath the casual conversation, the group has been dealing with some very important issues. The first was the matter of *inclusion.* You weren't the only one with questions going through your mind. Each one of the others was asking himself: *Do I want to be in this group? Do the others want me to be in the group? Is there anything I can do to make people want me?* The issue of inclusion was the same for everybody, but each person had a different way of dealing with the need to be accepted. You withheld information because you thought that if the others knew more about you they would reject you. Joan offered the magazine article in an attempt to make herself valuable to the group. Someone else may have been overly revealing. Perhaps another member wanted to become part of the group but unconsciously expected to get kicked out, so he behaved in an obnoxious way to make the group reject him and confirm his unconscious image of himself.

Now you're beginning to understand how the group process works. You have actually seen the way psychological hangups can influence behavior. And when nine other people tell you that they think you're holding back because you're afraid of rejection, it's pretty hard for you to deny it—to yourself as well as to the others.

How tough are you?

Gradually, as each one of you begins to feel included (accepted), you become more aware of the group leader. You begin to wonder how capable she is. Is she tough enough to take on all of you? Some of you try to find out by testing her. Perhaps the leader suggests moving to another room down the hall. Some of the members agree and begin getting their things together. But a few begin to quibble. Why move when this room is quite comfortable? Why disrupt the group when everybody is getting to know everybody? And some just sit there, waiting for the debate to end, apparently willing to go along with either side. But just you wait—although these neutrals aren't testing the therapist's power right now, they'll do it later on by arriving late or leaving early.

What's really happening? Well, the leader is an *authority* figure, and before the group can go on to other things, each member must attempt to relate to that authority. The way in which a person does it reveals a lot about the person's problems.

Besides inclusion and authority, there are three other issues that will emerge during the life of the group.

We're alike

At first each group member's attention was on himself as he struggled to find his place among the others. Then their attention went to the leader. After the issues of inclusion and authority are worked through—meaning that the members have resolved their difficulties—their concern goes outward toward each other. They begin to comment on each other's behavior—at first cautiously, then directly, boldly.

"Jim, every time one of us says something about how hard it is to accept the reality of a situation, you always butt in and top the story. I don't like that, and I wish you would cut it out."

"Joan, we all have our problems, but you and your whining voice sound as if you'd been condemned to hell. Can't you be happy about anything?"

"Hey, Bill, I like the way you listen when I talk. You seem to hear what I leave out as well as what I say."

Soon there is a healthy give-and-take in the group, and along with it a feeling of *affection* for each other.

This give-and-take makes you feel more comfortable. You realize that no one is out to attack you. On the contrary, the others care about you, which is a wonderful experience. You find that you care about them, too. What's more, you're able to say so. One woman is chronically absent, and when she shows up one evening you tell her how you feel.

"Mary," you say, "you may not realize it, but when you fail to show up, you hurt me—because I care about what happens to you."

And Mary's eyes open wide in amazement. She didn't know

anyone felt that way about her—and it makes a difference. Quiet, mousey Mary finally begins to open up a little—but in her case, that's a lot.

As more of you begin to risk revealing more about yourselves and your problems, you begin to see that you do have some similar ways of coping with life. It makes all of you feel good to be able to share your difficulties, to feel that there are others just like you after all. You even sense a kinship with those who don't speak up—you understand how they feel.

I'm different

But the feeling of oneness doesn't last. Something else takes its place. It's called *individuation*. Yes, you still feel affection for the other group members, and you still recognize some similarities. But you're also becoming aware of ways in which you are different from the others. And this is okay! In fact, you feel very good about it.

"You're very opinionated," Joe remarks, smiling with amusement at something you just said.

At first the comment shakes you up. If what he says is true, then it separates you from the group, and you feel a bit panicky. You stop and think a moment. You were going to deny vigorously that you were opinionated, but a tiny bell sounds in your head, telling you that, yes, what Joe said *is* true. You *are* opinionated.

And it's all right to be that way! That's the way you are! The important thing is that you realize it. It's all right with you if little Mary is a quiet person and Joan is pushy. That's the way *they* are.

So from then on you become fascinated with the discovery of your individual self. You don't have to hide the real you anymore. The group will accept you, warts and all. Even more important, you accept yourself—and that's something you can take with you beyond the group.

By now you have been in the group for a long time, perhaps as long as a year. When you break for a month during the summer, you feel pretty good about yourself, and you may even contemplate not returning in the fall. Maybe it's time for you to make it on your own. But a month later you're only too happy to get back to your "family." You've missed them. You've missed the give-and-take, and especially the way you can say whatever you feel in their presence. The outside world certainly isn't like that.

But that's exactly what you're going to talk about now—the outside world. It shook you up a bit to discover how unprepared you were to make relationships beyond the group. You know that eventually you must achieve that goal, so you share your anxiety. You find that the other group members had different versions of the same experience, depending upon the severity of their problems and the degree to which they had gained some insight into themselves.

So you have your work cut out for you during the next several months. Actually, the group experience requires about two years on the average, although some linger longer and others leave earlier. A few go on and on, never getting to the point where they feel they can assume their independence.

And now—good-bye

One Thursday morning you wake up horrified. You forgot to go to the group meeting last night! How could you do such a thing!

You wonder how you're going to live until next week's meeting, but as the days go by you begin to feel more comfortable with your oversight. You did survive, and you begin to realize that you are ready to think about leaving the group altogether. It isn't something you want to do right away. Give yourself time to change your mind. Maybe you're just cocky. Maybe you'll fall flat on your face without the group. Maybe the old problems will return and you'll feel miserable again.

But, no—the apprehensions don't stand up very long. You really are ready to face life on your own. You've learned to accept your feelings of guilt and resentment, and now you want to do something about getting out of the family business. You feel you can handle your own needs more directly now that you realize what they are.

Some of the other members are showing signs of what is called *termination*. It's a sad yet joyful time.

At one of the meetings you simply know that the time has come. And you say good-bye. You know you can come back if you need help, and perhaps you will continue individual sessions with your therapist.

Funny—it's like saying good-bye to your family.

Of course it is—because that's what actually has happened to you. That's the group process.

Inclusion, authority, affection, individuation, termination—these are the issues we face in life, from birth to maturity. The newborn baby is concerned with his inclusion in the family. Will he be fed and protected? Then he has to deal with authority during the age called "the terrible twos." Just how strong are these parents of his? From about four to ten or eleven, the child and his parents are on very affectionate terms, but during early adolescence, as the young person strives for his own identity—his individuation—there is stress. Finally, in late adolescence, the child moves out on his own, terminating his dependent relationship with his parents.

That's if all goes well. And it doesn't always.

Sometimes we are unsuccessful in dealing with one or more of these stages in life. We may even get stuck in one place indefinitely. That's why people go to group therapy, where they have an opportunity to reexperience the turning points that lead to maturity, and, hopefully, to work through the difficulties that began much earlier in life.

A fringe benefit of group psychotherapy is that it costs a lot less than individual psychotherapy: anywhere from twenty to thirty dollars per group session instead of from thirty-five to seventy-five dollars per individual session.

MARRIAGE GROUPS

"We do"

Psychotherapeutic groups deal with problems, but not always with specific problems such as obesity, addiction, alienation, depression, and the many others that can be caused by an inability to deal successfully with life's critical issues at an earlier age. The specific-problem-solving kind of group is very popular. Perhaps the most common one you will find is the group for married couples or couples living together.

If you and your mate are having problems, perhaps you will see a psychotherapist for a time. Probably he will point out that the two of you aren't communicating with each other very effectively and will give you some exercises to improve your ability to get your messages through to the other person. He may tell you to spend at least ten minutes each day talking to each other about your feelings—no other topic allowed! Now that may not sound like a lot of time to spend talking to each other, but I have news for you: The average couple talk to each other—really *talk* and *listen* to each other—for about three and a half minutes a day! The rest of the time they may jabber on for hours, but they really aren't getting through to each other in any meaningful way. So when you and your mate begin to take on a ten-minute conversation, it may seem like an eternity at first. But keep trying—you'll *like* it!

Your therapist also may instruct you to spend ten more minutes daily writing a note to each other. That may seem like two eternities at first—but only at first. Once you begin to open up to each other you may write a book.

Eventually your therapist may suggest that you join one of his couples groups, where you'll have a chance to find out what kind of problems other couples have and how they try to cope with them.

So you join the group, and immediately you begin to wonder whether you ought to be there at all. You don't want to leave, but your problems seem so small compared to the others. Inclusion again!

Yes, you will run into some of the same processes you find in any effective, well-structured, well-led group. But in addition there are some other advantages strictly for people who live together, married or not. For one thing, the other couples will draw your attention to some things about your behavior you hadn't noticed before. And then, you and your partner will have a chance to see each other in relationship to other individuals in the groups—and you may find that you really didn't know each other very well. This is very important, because one of the big problems in any close relationship is one partner's tendency to project upon the other only what he or she feels. Objectivity is a great problem-solver.

As you observe the ways in which other couples attempt to deal with their problems, you may begin to feel that you and your partner are able to deal with yours much more effectively than you realized. Or, if your relationship is a new one, you may feel more confident that it is off to a good start. Sometimes, however, a couple make the unhappy discovery that they are unable to live together comfortably. In that case, the group can help them work through their feelings of pain, guilt, and resentment so that they do not carry them through to another relationship.

ENCOUNTER GROUPS

There are groups and there are groups, and one of the biggest mistakes you can make is to lump them all together.

Group psychotherapy is one thing—but don't confuse it with encounter groups.

Frankly . . .

Let's say it's the beginning of your weekend of encounter with eleven people you've never met before. For forty-eight hours, interspersed with naps, snacks, and periods of relaxation, you will attempt to find out who you really are.

It wasn't a problem somewhere in your unconscious that led you to join the group. You know very well what your problem is: You just can't let go and be yourself. Specifically, you can't come right out and get angry with someone, no matter how justified you feel your anger may be. You're afraid the other person will refuse to have anything more to do with you. The other side of the coin is that you can't warm up to someone, either, no matter how much affection you feel inside. That's where your feelings stay—inside.

As the group begins, the leader asks you to tell the others your first name only. Don't mention what kind of work you do or where you live. Just give your first name and describe how you feel about being in the group.

That doesn't sound difficult, but actually it is. First of all, you don't feel comfortable in the group. Too many people are trying to talk at once, and the leader, called the *facilitator*, doesn't seem to have the group under control. But you don't want to say that. After all, you don't know these people.

Then Susan, another member of the group, says almost exactly what you were thinking, and what a relief it is! You speak up and tell the group you agree with Susan. It's a pretty aimless group, and you wish it could get started in some direction.

Carl disagrees. He claims this is the way a group should function. It must be free to go in any direction.

You're on the verge of telling Carl that he's a pompous ass, and what would he know about how the group should work anyway? But you don't quite dare.

Finally the facilitator breaks in to suggest that each person tell the group how he feels about the comments that were just made. And she begins with you.

Well, you shift uncomfortably and try to get off with a polite statement. No good.

"You sounded very angry," Susan says. "In fact, your face was contorted with anger. So you *must* have been angry, right?"

"A little," you falter.

"Then *say so!*" Susan demands.

The whole group backs her up, accusing you of holding back, of not being frank—which you agreed to be when you joined the group. They're playing rough. Some of the things they're saying about you are getting to you. You can't help yourself—you cry. And that makes you angrier than ever.

"Yes, I'm angry!" you bellow through your tears. "I'm mad as hell! Who do you think you are, ganging up on me? Some of you felt the same way I did—why didn't *you* say something?"

Now they're smiling. The whole group—and the leader—are smiling at you as if you were their most precious darling.

Why?

Because you were honest with them. It took a lot of prodding, but finally you let your anger out—and the world didn't cave in! In fact, the world applauded.

React to me

This is how encounter groups work. Their aim is not to solve your problems but to enable you to experience yourself through your interactions with other members of the group.

The very lack of structure in the beginning of the meeting was deliberate. Yes, it was uncomfortable, but it elicited some emotional reactions. Each of you began to realize that you were hiding behind a façade, suppressing your real feelings. But as you clashed with each other, some of the façade got chipped away. Eventually there you stood, totally exposed.

So long as you are a member of the group you have no choice but to participate. Unlike group psychotherapy, where members may remain silent, everyone in an encounter group is drawn out into the open and compelled to express himself. Sometimes this can be a very painful experience for the person in the "hot seat," and it is one of the reasons why encounter groups have attracted some sharp criticism.

The result, however—say the encounter therapists—is worth the pain, because once the person is forced to reveal himself, he sees that there is nothing to fear. Feelings he thought were taboo become desirable, applaudable, simply because they are expressed.

Encounter methods, however, are not recommended for persons with severe emotional disorders, because the demolition of their psychological defenses may cause serious trauma. Such persons have to be led more gently into self-awareness, and usually some supportive therapy is needed along the way.

Once the façades are stripped away, the group members begin to react to each others' revealed selves, sometimes in tones of antagonism, sometimes affectionately.

"I don't get the feeling that you give a damn about me," Carl says to you. "I've been watching your face while I'm talking, and you're like a stone. Nothing registers."

You try to explain that you really do care. In fact, you care about everyone in the group—more than you thought you ever could.

"Then why don't you show it?" Carl demands. "I was talking about something very painful to me—and if you do give a damn, why don't you *do* something?"

"Do what?" you ask. You desperately want to break through this barrier between you and those you want to approach.

"What do you feel like doing?" Carl asks.

Suddenly you take the plunge. You know very well what you feel like doing, and this time you're not going to ignore it. You're going to act on your feeling.

"I want to put my arms around you and comfort you," you say.

"Then *do* it!" someone shouts.

So you do. You hang on to your feeling and allow it to lead you. You stand up, walk over to Carl, and gently put your arms around him. You can actually feel his hurt, and you want to soothe it with your whole being. You begin to rock him back and forth, and before you know it the two of you are sobbing.

"I feel your caring," Carl says.

"And I feel your pain," you tell him.

You also feel tremendous relief at being able to express what you feel.

At the end of your forty-eight hours together, you and the other members of the group are no longer strangers. You are closer to each other than you are to your own families. You know a lot about each other and much more about yourselves. Hopefully, you will take that knowledge back into the world with you and allow it to lead you into richer relationships with those around you.

PEER GROUPS

If you have a compulsive problem, such as drinking, smoking, overeating, gambling, taking drugs, or any of the other addictions, you may find a peer group helpful. By *peer* I mean a group in which all members share the same problem. Alcoholics Anonymous is a well-known example.

Usually there is no charge for these groups and there is no therapist per se. Each member becomes a therapist to the other members in that he shares his experiences and offers his encouragement and support to them in their efforts to overcome their problems. He also depends on the others to support him.

The value of the peer group is that each member knows what it is to have "been there." Each is familiar with the typical excuses for backsliding into dependency on a habit and with the behavior patterns associated with it. They are not easily fooled by pretenses, and while they are compassionate, they are tough about the self-discipline required to fight a compulsion.

Usually a peer group meets once a week, but all members are on call for help and support at any hour of the day or night. The weekly meetings of some groups resemble a tent revival meeting in some respects, as member after member stands up and talks about his problem. The purpose here is to encourage a person to face the reality of his compulsion, to admit that he has a problem and needs help in solving it. Any drift into self-pity is quickly interrupted and blocked by the other members.

Some groups use encounter methods of confrontation, which are particularly effective in dealing with a person who wants to avoid taking responsibility for his problem. Most groups encourage their members to set strict goals for themselves, which usually means giving up their compulsive habits for as long as possible. Backsliding and despair are frequent and painful, but the person who feels he will never succeed in overcoming his problem is constantly reassured of eventual success by the presence of others who have achieved it.

Many peer groups believe that a compulsive dependency on a habit is never completely eliminated, and for this reason they consider membership to be permanent. Others believe that once a problem is understood and solved, a person should be able to get along on his own—although they stand ready to readmit anyone who feels he needs continued or occasional support.

NUDE MARATHON

Don't let anyone tell you that nude marathon therapy is the same as encounter group therapy but without clothes. Believe me, there *is* a difference.

The nude marathon lasts for twenty-four hours, sometimes forty-eight (average cost is sixty to one hundred and twenty dollars), and its aim is not to help you improve your ability to relate to others on a deeper level—although this ultimately happens after a successful marathon experience—but to unlock emotions buried deep within you. Like encounter group therapy, however, it is most effective with persons who have difficulty in their relationships, in expressing their emotions, and in achieving intimacy.

What are you covering up?

If you were to attend a nude marathon, you would begin the session early in the evening. Your group would include about fourteen to eighteen men and women of different ages and backgrounds.

You would begin with your clothes on.

The first thing your therapist would ask you all to do is have *eyeball contact*, meaning that, one by one, you are to look directly into each member's eyes—without speaking. Then, still not speaking, you would go on to physical contact —hugging, wrestling, touching, whatever your spontaneous desire is at the moment. There is only one restriction, and this is constant throughout the marathon: no erotic contact.

Then it is time to talk, and the subject is your anxiety over appearing nude. As all of you reveal your concerns about it, your anxiety begins to diminish.

Now the room is darkened and soft music can be heard. You and the others disrobe, and then the therapist tells you all to walk in a small circle, with your eyes closed. You begin to feel the closeness of the others. You feel your nudity before you actually see it, and by the time you see each other in the light you are more comfortable with yourself.

If you haven't loosened up yet, you'll be given an exercise to finish off any lingering inhibitions. The group is told to lie down on the floor and form a circle. Then each one lifts his legs in the air and looks at the others through his legs. It's okay to laugh.

While you're still in this position, you are asked to tell the group about any sexual experiences that have left you with a feeling of guilt. In other words, you are supposed to tell everyone some of your innermost secrets—because when you do you will realize that even though the group sees you in this ridiculous position and knows the worst about you, they still accept you. And that's a great relief! It also is the beginning of trust between you and the other members.

About four hours have gone by. For the next four hours you will meditate and sleep. (You were asked to bring a sleeping bag with you.)

Becoming an infant

Now you are being led to a pool which is heated to body temperature (98.6 degrees). You are told not to speak to each other, but to communicate in any nonverbal way that is comfortable.

One by one you are taken into the pool by the other members of the group. And one by one you are rocked gently in the warm, shallow water. All over your body you feel the contact of other human beings who are massaging your muscles wherever your physical tension is evident. Perhaps you are a little fearful that they will let your head sink beneath the water. You tense up. Immediately the loving hands are there, soothing the rigid muscles and easing the pain caused by your tension.

Now you hear your favorite music, and perhaps the scent of something you particularly like—perfume, incense, a flower—is detectable. You feel yourself relaxing a bit more. You feel you really can trust the others to hold your head above the water.

The therapist is urging you to talk now, to tell the group whatever you are beginning to recall about your early childhood, or your infancy—even your birth! Because you *can* remember these things.

You see, the marathon processes have been helping you to regress to that early time in your life. Like a newborn baby, you are naked. You are in a physical environment reminiscent of the womb, where you are wet and warm, nourished, held, rocked, and protected. You have been communicating without the use of words, the way a baby does.

In fact, you have become yourself as an infant. You remember things you never could have remembered before. Loving touches, fears, anxieties, anger—often all of them related to the same person, such as a parent. The emotional contradictions are confusing.

As you express the trust you knew as a child, you become more aware of the closeness of the other group members. You feel the comfort of their massaging hands and the strength of their arms holding you, rocking you back and forth as if you were an infant. But as you recall some of the rages you felt, you are offered a cushion to strike at as hard as you can. Whatever you feel, you can express in perfect trust and confidence.

And perhaps you remember suddenly that you loved your mother very much when you were an infant. But then, when you were three years old, she died, and you hated her for abandoning you. So alternately you caress and you strike out, and finally you realize that your rage is childish. You allow yourself to forgive your mother for leaving you, which gives you a sense of deep inner peace.

As the marathon continues, you become one of the loving, supporting members, and you see others cry and scream and exult with a newly discovered ability to love. Each one is different. Each has his own memories. And each is renewed by his ability to call them forth from the darkness of the past.

The marathon is over now, but you feel like a different person. You feel you can trust others, get closer to them, allow them to get close to you. Perhaps when you go home your spouse notices the difference and is also able to communicate on a more intimate level. Perhaps the women and men with whom you work express a new warmth in response to your own capacity for intimacy.

You didn't attend the marathon in the expectation of changing your life. Yet your life is changing. Your values are different, and now you must adapt your lifestyle to those values. But that's all right. Because it's going to be better that way.

FAMILY THERAPY

A relatively new and effective method of helping people to solve their problems is family therapy. As its name implies, it means that an entire family—not a representation of it—is treated by one or more therapists.

Immediately one imagines a whole family converging upon a therapist's office and seeking help—which isn't exactly what happens. Usually a mother brings her child to a psychotherapist because the child is emotionally disturbed. Perhaps he is having trouble in school and several teachers have recommended professional help.

The therapist begins by seeing the child and then has several consultations with the mother. It soon becomes apparent to the therapist that at least part of the child's problem is connected in some way to a difficulty in the mother's relationship with her husband, and so the therapist then attempts to consult with the child's father. By then the therapist senses that if one child is having problems, the other children in the family also may be having them, with less visible manifestations. Finally the therapist meets with the entire family—including grandparents, aunts, uncles, even cousins—in his office. This goes on for several weeks. Eventually the scene shifts to the family's home, with perhaps more than one therapist observing their interactions.

Connectedness

The theory underlying family therapy is that the ills of the individual may very well be related to, or caused by, his interrelationship with other members of his family. He may, in fact, be expressing someone else's pain. Consequently, the best way to discover the causes of the ills is to understand all the members of the family and how they relate to each other—and the best place to solve the problems resulting from these ills is in the midst of family life.

Consider for a moment the individual patient discussing his problems with his therapist. Suppose he gains some insight into his difficulty and begins to change his approach to life and to those around him. Naturally this is going to bring on some changes in the way his family responds to him—and when this happens, all hell can break loose. Some families fight any change in any of the family members, some become too involved in the new experiences of the person undergoing psychotherapy and attempt to manipulate him, and some may even have violent reactions to his improvement simply because it threatens their established relationship to him.

Now consider the person who had the original problem.

True, he won't feel that his therapist is strictly on his side. And he won't be able to concentrate solely on his own problems and needs. But because his therapist (or therapists) will be dealing with all the problems and relationships within the family, changes in his behavior will be incorporated with changes in the responses of others to him.

How?

The method is more behavioral than psychoanalytic, by necessity and for reasons of practicality. As the therapists study the family interactions in the family's home, they note the causes and effects of gestures, facial expressions, tone of voice, choice of words, body language. They begin to see a pattern of behavior emerging. Perhaps a mother constantly indulges a son in the presence of his father, which arouses the father's antagonism toward the son. Perhaps a daughter sides with her mother in ridiculing the father. Perhaps a child who is ignored by one parent attempts to imitate that parent in order to understand him. Families are complicated and the possibility for problems is endless.

Once the therapists determine what is happening to cause the obvious difficulty, they begin to work with all the family members on changing the way they behave toward each other. The changes are small at first, because one change makes a big difference to everyone. A mother who interrupts a daughter consistently will be made aware of her behavior, and the daughter may be asked to write her mother notes for a period of time. This enables the daughter to experience the relief of completing her communication and it breaks up the mother's habit of interrupting.

Family therapy is a book in itself and much too complicated to go into here. But it is fascinating and it is growing in importance, especially in these times, when the American family seems to be falling apart and is evidently in need of help. The important thing about it is that it *does* work in stabilizing a family that may otherwise disintegrate, and this is of great value in a social sense.

Two buts . . .

But—not everyone with a problem, or a problem child, is a candidate for family therapy. Persons with a strong sense of individuality will resist having to downplay their own progress for the sake of the group, and this is a definite drawback of this therapy. It works best with families of schizophrenic children, in most of whom there is little sense of themselves as individuals.

Another But is that family therapy is much too expensive for most people if it is practiced privately. Usually it isn't. If you want to find a family therapist, you will probably have to go to a public health center or a hospital clinic. At the moment, and probably into the foreseeable future, these methods are more often available to the disadvantaged, who, in the long run, are those with the greatest need for it.

CHAPTER 6
HYPNOTHERAPY

Hypnotherapy is the modern word for hypnosis. While hypnosis has been around for several centuries, scientific research into the process began only about forty years ago. And with the research came some long-delayed respect for the results that could be achieved through hypnosis. Hence the suffix *therapy*, which is science's way of saying, yes, hypnosis *can* help a person get better.

The late, late show

But you—what do you know about hypnosis? Probably not much at all. If you're like most people—I know I was—the little you know comes from watching old movies on TV. You know the routine: The person being hypnotized is told to look at a flickering candle flame or a dangling watch while the hypnotist—a glary-eyed character with a pasty complexion and obviously sinister intent—says over and over, "Sleep, you're going to sleep . . . deeper and deeper you're falling, falling into a deep sleep . . ." You just know he's up to no good, and pretty soon he goes on to prove it.

Beyond the nonsense

The old movie versions of hypnosis are a lot of hogwash.

There is nothing magical, mystical, or sinister about hypnosis. In fact, it can be extremely helpful in relieving and even curing certain kinds of problems.

A person in a hypnotic trance cannot be made to do something she would not do in her natural state. So don't be afraid you'll make a fool of yourself or allow the therapist to take advantage of you.

And if your therapist should suddenly die or go off on a long vacation, leaving you still in a hypnotic trance, don't worry. You'll come back to reality all by yourself in a very short time. It simply is not possible to remain stuck in a hypnotic trance.

As for going berserk emotionally, it just doesn't happen. One of the aims of hypnosis is to keep the subject calm so that he can be more receptive to therapy. Also, even while in a trance, you won't take on any more emotion than you can handle.

So there. Hopefully that gets rid of the nonsense.

But if so, then what *is* hypnosis?

It is, says Dr. William S. Kroger, one of the foremost practitioners and authorities on hypnosis, the systematic use of some perfectly natural functions of the brain—functions which occur in our everyday life.

Have you ever driven along a highway for a long time? You know what happens—the constant whirring of the wheels on the pavement, the never-ending long black strip before you, sitting in one position for hours. After a while you feel yourself slipping into a sleeplike state—and you shake your head sharply to pull out of it, because this is no place to go into a trance.

What happened to you?

Quite simply, you began to relax because what you saw and heard were so repetitious and dull. There was nothing to distract you, so your attention began to focus on the scenery and the sounds, closing out the rest of the world. That's a form of hypnosis—and you do it by yourself.

Want a posthypnotic suggestion?

You're watching TV and along comes a soap commercial you've seen many times before. So you dash into the kitchen to get a cup of coffee and come back in time to catch the rest of the show. But the next time you're in the supermarket and reach for a box of soap, what kind do you buy? The one in the commercial you've seen so many times. You almost can't help yourself, because when you were in a relaxed state, watching TV, you were repeatedly told to buy a certain product.

Have you ever momentarily forgotten your own telephone number? Or your own name? Or the name of your best friend as you were about to introduce her to someone else? These are only brief lapses, but they do happen to us all, and it doesn't mean there is anything wrong. It means our minds were focused on something else at the time.

Sleepwalking is another example. Some people can walk around with their eyes wide open and even carry on a conversation—yet they are asleep. Or, rather, their minds are asleep.

You know the old expression "My mind plays tricks on me"? Well, it isn't quite accurate. You see, our minds don't actually play tricks on us, but sometimes they aren't in the same place as we are. They're somewhere else. And this is what the hypnotist tries to control. He tries to relax everything about the subject except the subject's mind.

A hypnotherapist may use something as simple as a beautiful painting of a calm, peaceful scene and ask the person to look at it as she tries to relax. Gradually the therapist will lead the person to concentrate on the scene until she begins to close out everything else around her.

Or a hypnotherapist may not use anything at all. He may talk the person into a state of complete relaxation, or perhaps he will offer a comfortable vibrating chair to make the person more comfortable.

No candles, no dangling watch, no drugs. Simply relaxation.

Then the therapy begins. It is relatively quick, and in most instances can be completed in a few sessions. Costs vary greatly, anywhere from ten to fifty dollars a session.

Believing makes it so

A hypnotherapist will tell you that he doesn't actually put anyone into a trance. It's the subject who does it to himself through some of the natural brain functions we just discussed. The hypnotherapist must have the subject's confidence so that he allows his brain functions to come under the therapist's control and direction. The subject must have such faith in the therapist and the therapy that he expects to be helped by them. The therapist then cooperates with the subject's expectation.

Here is an example of how that cooperation works:

A middle-aged woman was being examined for possible brain damage, and one of her complaints was that she was extremely forgetful. When one of the doctors attending her asked her to multiply three times seventeen in her head, she became very nervous.

"Three times seven is twenty-one," she began, ". . . oh, three times seven is twenty-one, and—I can't do it!" She said she could not hold the 1 and carry the 2 while finishing the multiplication.

"Is there any way I can help you?" one of the doctors asked.

"Yes," she said, smiling hopefully. "You can hold the numbers for me."

She began again. "Three times seven is twenty-one . . ." She turned to the doctor and held out her hand to him. "Now you hold the one and the two," she said.

"Next, three times one is three," she went on, "plus the two you are holding, which makes five. Five and the one you are holding makes fifty-one . . . so three times seventeen is fifty-one!"

The doctor "holding" the numbers didn't actually do anything except cooperate with her illusion of being helped. But, under this illusion, the woman was able to do things she was otherwise unable to do.

How you can be helped

Hypnosis is a flexible therapy that can be used for several different types of problems.

Relaxation: If you are an especially tense person, hypnosis can put you into a state of deep rest. After a few sessions you will notice an improvement in your physical condition because the deep rest is counteracting the destructive effects of tension. Eventually you will be able to put yourself into a trance whenever you need relaxation, and in this way you will gain a sense of control over your tension. The security of this control may help you to gain some insight into whatever is causing your problems.

Symptom suppression: While you are in a trance, your therapist will tell you to stop behaving in a certain way. For instance, if you want to stop smoking he will tell you that smoking is bad for your health, that it is a filthy habit and you must stop it right away.

Although hypnotherapy is not a long process, don't get the idea that you will be able to stop smoking after one session. Depending upon the subject, several sessions may be needed.

Anesthetic: Your doctor or dentist may use hypnosis as a natural anesthetic against pain.

Uncovering: Sometimes it is not enough to suppress a symptom (such as phobias or shyness). The cause must be found (*uncovering*) and the pent-up emotions released (*catharsis*).

One of the most interesting cases was that of a young woman who went to a party with her husband and became very angry when her husband drank too much. Some of her thoughts at that moment were so hateful that they frightened her, and she repressed them.

Later that night, as the couple were driving home, the husband passed out at the wheel and the car crashed into a tree. The husband was killed, but the wife came through without a scratch. But she couldn't remember the accident, and she was terrified of leaving her house, because she thought some terrible force would strike her dead.

Under hypnosis the woman was able to remember all the events of the evening her husband died. She remembered how angry she had been, angry enough to wish him dead.

Slowly the therapist led the woman back over all her feelings before the accident (uncovering) and encouraged her to express them (catharsis). Then, as he led her to the memory of the accident itself, he pointed out to her that her husband's death was not her fault and was in no way a consequence of her anger toward him. When the trance was ended, the therapist then helped the woman to understand how the fear of her own anger had caused her to feel responsible for her husband's death. Once she realized that the two were not connected, she was able to recover from her terror of leaving her house.

A word of caution

Hypnosis is not a difficult or a complicated procedure. Almost anyone can learn to do it effectively. But not anyone can help a person make good use of the things she may learn through hypnosis. That takes training beyond the ability to induce a trance in a willing subject.

In hypnotherapy, as in behavior therapy, you will learn new ways to respond to certain stimuli, and this can be very helpful—but only if your therapist knows how to teach you what to do with your new responses and how to integrate them into the rest of your life.

No matter which therapy you choose, it is important to seek out a thoroughly qualified therapist. But in hypnotherapy it is especially important. Be sure that the person you consult is trained in the *therapy* as well as the *hypno* part of the word.

CHAPTER 7
PRIMAL THERAPY

Before you can be accepted for Primal Therapy, you must have a complete physical examination and be declared physically sound. You must also write a short history of your life and family, and indicate why you want to go into therapy. The reason for this kind of screening is that Primal Therapy is a rugged experience.

It is sometimes called Primal *Scream* Therapy.

That first Scream

In the late sixties, during a clinical group therapy session, Dr. Arthur Janov, a California psychiatrist, watched a twenty-two-year-old man writhing in agony on the floor. Only a few moments earlier, the young man had mentioned a play he had seen in which one of the adult characters cried out, "Mommy! Daddy!" to his parents, just as though he were a child. Following a hunch, Dr. Janov asked his patient to do the same thing.

From the beginning the patient was visibly upset. His breathing became rapid and irregular. His cries to his parents became screeches. Janov thought he might be going into a coma. Then, after a series of convulsions, the patient uttered "a piercing, deathlike scream that rattled the walls of my office"—and became quiet.

A few minutes later the patient reported that at last he was in touch with his feelings and could express them comfortably, something which had not been possible before. He had no ill-effects from the experience and felt fine. He couldn't explain what had happened, and neither could Dr. Janov. But Janov sensed that it was the beginning of something important.

It was. That first scream was the beginning of Primal Therapy (the capital letters are Janov's). And the therapy came before the theory which later was its foundation.

Janov began to use the same kind of therapy on other patients, and their responses were similar to the young man's. As each one cried out to his parents, the cries became screams of pain, and the patients' voices and bodies took on the characteristics of a very young child. Janov concluded that the screams came from the accumulation of hurts inflicted during the patient's infancy and childhood. These he called Primal Pains. The Primal Scream, as he called it, was the result of forcing the patient to relive the experiences which had caused the Pain.

So now there was a theory . . .

As Janov describes it, every child has natural needs for love, reassurance, protection, attention. When any of these needs are not met, the child begins to feel that the needs must be bad, and that he himself must be bad for having them. The need therefore becomes equated with the self—the "I" of the child. But also there are demands which the parents make upon the child, and if these are met, the parents' approval makes the child feel he is doing something good; therefore *he* must be good. Neurosis, says Janov, occurs when the child becomes less and less his real self and more and more what he thinks others, particularly his parents, want him to be. His real self, and its natural needs, becomes split off, locked away, eventually not even remembered, while his unreal self shapes his behavior and personality.

For example, suppose a very young child is asked to take on adult responsibilities in her family. Perhaps her parents, out of their own unmet infant needs, expect her to look after them and comfort them. The child, needing these things herself, resists at first. But when her dependency and unwillingness to take charge meet with constant disapproval, she feels herself drawn to the behavior her parents demand of her.

Each time the child's own need for love is shunned, she experiences Pain, and as the Pain increases it becomes unbearable. Finally the child's real feelings become separated from her consciousness. This split may be caused by a particularly traumatic event, which Janov calls the Primal Scene, or by the infliction of one too many Pains upon the child, causing her to feel that her parents hate her. This she cannot endure, so she pushes her real needs into the background. From that moment a false self begins to emerge, a self willing to become a kind of prostitute for her parents' approval.

"I will act like the little parent you want me to be—anything to get love from you," she is saying.

This attempt to please one's parents, and later people in general, is called the Struggle, because a person cannot simply put her real needs aside and assume another self. She must struggle to become the person others want her to be. In time she will become more adept in the role; eventually it will seem natural to her. She will become, as Janov puts it, "more unreal than real."

But that isn't the end of the Struggle. It continues on the unconscious level as long as the person's real needs are denied, and those needs will seek fulfillment in other ways. The child whose parents forced her to take charge at an early age will become an adult looking for substitute parents to take care of her. Perhaps, like her own parents, she will make the same unreasonable demands of her children. Of course, she will be fulfilling her needs only symbolically—and that will never be enough.

Back to the source of the Pain

Primal therapists believe that neurosis can be cured only by going back to the Primal Pain itself. It is not enough for a person to understand the reasons for her behavior, because the problem is one of *feeling* and must be solved on the emotional level. In fact, as PT therapists point out, so much neurotic adult behavior is the result of an attempt to avoid feeling that intellectualizing the problem only prolongs this attempt. Instead, the person must be forced by the therapy to meet the problem head on. She must relive the original hurts inflicted upon her by her parents, release the agony pent up inside her, and finally free herself of it.

As you can see, the process is not comfortable. Many authorities consider it better suited to people who have severe feelings of alienation and whose lack of contact with their deeper emotions makes it almost impossible for them to form relationships or to express their needs. Since it also results in a major change in behavior and personality, it should be considered only by those persons willing to undergo changes which cannot be predicted in advance. It is not recommended for persons who are easily influenced by suggestion, or for those with a specific problem to solve. Primal Therapy is a breakthrough method rather than a problem-solving procedure. Its aim is to contact the emotions rather than to adapt them to life situations.

Becoming able to Scream

If you were to go into Primal Therapy, for the first three weeks you would not go to work or to school or to wherever you normally do during your daily routine. Your therapy must be the only thing of importance in your life. You would have to pay, in advance, from thirty-five hundred to six thousand dollars for the entire process, which lasts from six to eight months.

For the first twenty-four hours you would stay in a hotel room. Alone. You would not be permitted to read, watch television, smoke, take drugs or alcohol. But you would be permitted to write. The reason for this isolation is to deprive you of any of your usual outlets for tension, giving you no alternative but to face your feelings, however muddled they may be. If your defenses seemed to be particularly strong, you would be told not to sleep for these twenty-four hours, which would deprive you of the opportunity to act out your unreal self in your dreams.

Yes, you would be nervous, anxious, and tired. And that would be good.

Your first session with your therapist might shake you up a bit. Probably you will be expecting him to say or do something to put you at ease. Well, he won't. He won't tell you to relax or give you sympathy or tell you that you'll soon feel better. He will tell you to lie down on a mat in a spread-eagled position, which in itself is going to make you feel extremely vulnerable. He will ask you to talk about how you *feel*. If you laugh, complain, or try to analyze your reactions, he'll tell you to stop.

For the first three weeks of therapy you would see your therapist every day for several hours at a time, depending upon how much he thought you could handle. You would be the only patient he would see during those weeks.

You and your therapist would discuss what was bothering you, but briefly. Your therapist would want to know about your early life, not the present, and he would keep hammering away at your resistance to recall. You would insist that you can't remember back so far, and he would insist that you can. If you remembered that you were afraid of your father, your therapist would ask you to call out to your father and tell him about your fear. That wouldn't be easy. You might refuse to do it at first. But gradually, as your defenses were worn away, you would try. And as you did, you would feel a rush of emotion. You would begin to remember exactly how you felt when you were a child—when you were only an infant. You might even remember being born, which in itself might have been a painful experience for you.

This rush of emotion and your attempt to hold it back is called a Pre-Primal, and it means you are making progress. It would happen again, with greater frequency, as you began to relive your distant past. Your voice would begin to change and so would your vocabulary until you sounded and spoke just as you did when you were very young. For, you see, you are becoming your real self again as an infant.

Perhaps your therapist would give you some exercises to do as he sensed you were approaching your Primal Scream. He might tell you to lie down and keep your mouth open as you tried to pull your feelings up from your gut. When you were able to do that, when you had the sensation that something was coming through from very deep within yourself, you would experience your first Primal Scream. It would feel as if your real self were breaking through the unreal self, and the more you screamed the more you would become aware of that natural, original you.

Once you had contact with your real self, you would experience more Screams, or Primals, as they are called—and more often. Beginning with the second week of therapy, they would occur almost daily as you dredged up more and more painful memories and gained new insights into their affect on your behavior. You might even have a few Primals by yourself.

It doesn't really hurt

A word about these Pains.

They don't really hurt. Not in the physical sense.

During the first few days of therapy you might have headaches, backaches, or other minor aches, but they would be caused by your tension. And your tension would be relieved when you began to have your Primals.

As for the Primals themselves, well, as Janov puts it, the more Pain you feel, the less pain you will have. Which is his way of saying that it is the blocked-up Pain that really hurts. Freeing it up is a great and beautiful relief. Janov's patients confirm this point of view and say that at the very moment they are Screaming they do not actually experience physical pain. In fact, they claim they can stop the Scream at any time, but that they do not want to.

Group Primals

After three weeks you would go into a form of group therapy. You wouldn't be expected to interact with the other members or to be deliberately supportive. Just do your own thing, which in this instance means having your Primals as often as necessary. The purpose of the group is to provide an atmosphere conducive to uninhibited release of Pain. It doesn't matter if another group member is Screaming—go right ahead and have your Scream along with her. In fact, the sight of others having their Primals may inspire more of your own.

You would meet with this group, under the leadership of your therapist, twice a week for at least three hours. How long you remain in the group would depend upon your individual progress, but figure on at least six months. By the end of eight months most patients are ready to leave, but some remain for as long as eleven months. You would know you were ready to leave when you could bring up your buried feelings on your own and without resistance. Patients who continue to raise defenses against experiencing deep feelings are not considered well.

The natural Person

No, you would not go on Screaming for the rest of your life. After your Pain had been released, you would have no need to Scream. Nor would you have any defenses—but, says Dr. Janov, you wouldn't need them, either. You would become a "natural" person, which means that your unreal self would have disintegrated.

Whether or not that "natural" self is desirable has been the subject of much debate about Primal Therapy. As Janov describes post-Primal patients, they are "non-industrial, non-compulsive and non-driving." Their need for sex is greatly diminished; in some patients it is down to once or twice a month. Some critics of Primal Therapy feel that recovered patients live so much in the here-and-now that they have no interest in what is going on in the rest of the world. They are said to be indifferent to achieving, striving, or struggling—content simply to exist, to feel, and to attempt to meet their "natural" needs.

Janov's answer to these criticisms is that such things as achieving, striving, and struggling are "symbolic substitutes," or neurotic cover-ups, for our real needs.

Who is right?

You'll have to decide that for yourself.

CHAPTER 8
PSYCHOANALYTIC THERAPY

You're confused. You have deep inner pain and you don't know why. It's interfering with your life.

You have a problem and you want to do something about it. But do you need psychoanalysis or psychoanalytic therapy?

What's the difference between the two? Or is there any?

Answering the second question first: Yes, there is a difference. *Psychoanalysis* is the application of a theory, and when you are psychoanalyzed you explore the deepest levels of your internal thoughts, feelings, and fantasies. But you do not solve problems, at least not directly. What you do with your acquired knowledge of yourself is up to you and is not part of the analysis. The process is primarily educational, and is therapeutic only in the sense that the more you know about yourself, the better you can deal with your problems.

Psychoanalytic therapy is a course of treatment based upon the principles of psychoanalysis, but it is problem-concerned. What you do with your knowledge of yourself and how you apply it to reality situations is very much a part of the therapy.

And there are other differences which we will go into shortly.

But before we do . . .

Schools of thought

There is more to psychoanalysis and psychoanalytic therapy than Sigmund Freud. He was the father, the founder, the developer of the psychoanalytic process, but the process did not stop with him. Freud's theories were revolutionary in his day, and it was he who first conceptualized the structure and components of psychoanalysis. It is largely his terminology we still use today, but there were and are many who disagreed with him about the causes of neurosis. And as these dissidents, many of whom had been his pupils and associates, became more outspoken, schools of psychoanalytic thought grew up around them. Today, when you seek out a psychotherapist, the treatment you undergo will depend to some extent upon the school of thought he favors.

Basically the divisions of thought arose over the interpretation of the causes of neurosis, Freud insisting they were biological (sexual) in nature and others contending that they were rooted in the structure of society, the person's early environment, or the way in which the person perceived reality. Some of the outstanding psychoanalytic schools of thought, besides that of Freud, are patterned after the developments of Karen Horney, Carl Jung, Harry Stack Sullivan, Alfred Adler, Otto Rank, William Alanson White, Theodore Reik, Erik Erikson, and Erich Fromm.

Space does not permit me to go into the theories of all these psychoanalytic giants, but since Sigmund Freud was the first and the founder, I think the reader needs to become familiar with his work. Bear in mind, however, that much of his thinking has been revised—sometimes by him at later dates, and sometimes by those who felt his views were too narrow.

A word about Sigmund Freud

It is very hard to put Freud in a nutshell. The man was too complex, too fascinating; his genius was too immense for the longest book, let alone a few paragraphs.

Still, let's give it a try.

Freud (1856–1939) spent most of his professional life in Vienna, where he began by studying medicine. In private practice he specialized in nervous disorders but was frustrated by the limited amount of knowledge available in his field. On his own he studied hypnosis and the effect of drugs on certain types of hysteria. Then he met Dr. Joseph Breuer, also a neurologist, who had developed a "talking therapy" in which patient and doctor verbally probed the patient's symptoms, looking for an underlying nonphysical cause. Freud and Breuer worked together for several years, improving on the talking therapy, but then had a falling-out over the significance of sexuality in nervous disorders. As you might have guessed, Freud emphasized the sexual basis of disorders, while Breuer did not.

On his own, Freud expanded the talking therapy from a simple exploration of the psyche into a penetrating analysis of what makes the psyche tick.

The result was psychoanalysis, a study which Freud continued for the rest of his life. Today, wherever psychoanalysis is practiced—and that is almost everywhere—it is based upon a theory very much like the one Freud developed.

For the first time in the history of the world, people were presented with a detailed picture of their inner selves, one which was not always complimentary and in many ways was shocking. So explosive was this information that the world has never been the same since, and you could almost draw a line between pre-Freudian and post-Freudian lifestyles. Nothing was untouched by its influence—art, literature, politics, business, education, war, medicine, and, above all, human relations were different after the introduction of Freud's psychoanalytic theory.

What's going on in your libido?

According to Freud, the energy for all our behavior comes from the *libido*, which is like a battery filled with positive and negative cells. The positive, creative, pleasure-loving elements (or cells, to carry on the analogy) are called eros, after the Greek god of sexual love, and, as you might imagine, this is where our sexual drive originates. The negative elements (cells) are called *thanatos*, which in Greek means *death*, and here is where our aggressive, destructive instincts reside. The two forces—life-loving sex and death, creativity and destruction, pleasure and hate—are constantly in conflict with each other, and the tension generated by their conflict is called *libido*.

Picture it this way: Eros says, "I want to build and love and have a good time." Thanatos says, "I want to destroy, hate, and wreak havoc." Sooner or later, something's got to give, right? Well, that "give" eventually becomes what we do, our behavior. In one way or another, that inner tension has to be released.

But first, other forces must get into the act.

Libido comes of age

When we are born, our libidinal energy comes into the world with us, but it goes through several stages of development, just as we do. As infants, and until we are about two years old, we begin to discover the world through our mouths, which become sensitized by our libidinous desires to experience pleasure. Given something she likes, the child swallows it and asks for more. But given something she finds distasteful, the child spits it out and begins to wail. (It's easy to see the eros and thanatos drives at work in that example.)

If there are disturbances in the child's development during this oral stage, she may get stuck there, becoming what is called "an oral-gratification character" even in adulthood. Some examples are heavy smokers, alcoholics, and compulsive eaters—people who, for one reason or another, never got enough libido satisfaction as infants and are still looking for it in symbolic forms.

When a child is about two years old the libido begins to sensitize the anal areas of her body, and both child and parents become preoccupied with toilet training. Here, Freud believed, the child got her pleasure from an unassisted bowel movement that in turn pleased her parents. But, as most parents know, the anal stage is a touchy time. Too much applause or too much disapproval over bowel movements, and the child grows up to become an "anal character": greedy, stingy, power-hungry, and stubborn—or sloppy, loud, mushy, overly philanthropic, depending upon whether the thanatos or eros instinct was demanding satisfaction.

From the age of three to about seven, we go through the *phallic stage*, a preview of the later genital stage, when we satisfy our pleasure instinct by fondling the genital areas of our body. This is when little boys experience unconscious incestuous desires for their mothers (the *Oedipal stage*) and little girls want their fathers (the *Electra stage*). In boys, this desire, when frustrated, is accompanied by a fear that the father will castrate them. So, as you can see, there is a conflict—one which is resolved when the boy begins to identify with his father and gives up his desires for his mother. (Eventually he will look for a female of his own.) As the girl begins to identify with her mother, she surrenders her longing for her father. (She will want her own male at a later age.)

From the age of six to eleven the child goes through the *latency stage*, so called because the libidinous forces seem rather quiet during these years. The child plays with other children of her own sex and becomes interested in games, school, and sports. Actually, however, she has repressed all memory of any sexual and hostile feelings toward her parents during the previous years. Yet those first five years will influence the rest of her development—*unconsciously*.

Finally the libido enters the *genital stage*. During the early times, boys begin to feel attracted to girls, and girls to boys. Here the child also becomes aware of her own sexuality.

Three little words: id, ego, and superego

Just about everybody I know uses these words in ordinary conversation, and just about everybody uses them incorrectly. I did too, for a long time, until my studies led me to their correct meaning.

You know how it goes—somebody says Joe has a big ego, meaning Joe is a vain guy who thinks only of himself. Then we talk about the id as something dark and mysterious—evil, almost. And the supergo, well, that's not as popular a word, but when most of us use it we mean some kind of schoolmarm, a regulator of sorts.

Quite wrong! And not very flattering to these three important parts of the human psyche. While they aren't exactly goody-goods, they aren't as bad as we usually paint them, either.

The *id* is the repository of the creative and destructive libidinous forces, and is the source of our psychic energy. Here is where all our I-wants originate. Now, some of those I-wants are rather shocking if we consider them out of context. "Am I *really* like that?" would be a perfectly natural reaction.

And the answer, according to Freud, is that, yes, *part* of you really is like that. But there is more to you than that one part.

For instance, there is your *ego*, which is your contact with reality. Your ego sees the possible consequences of what the id wants to do. It sees that you can't go on gobbling good-tasting food as long as you please, because after you have had enough your parents will deny you more. And if you cry and carry on, you may get spanked, or scolded, or ignored, or something else equally unpleasant. The ego sees that you can't have all your mother's attention, that you can't get rid of your father, that you can't get back at your parents by smearing your feces all over the bathroom or all over your clothes. The consequences would be too uncomfortable. So the ego says, "Hold on, Id, you can't do that," when the I-want is unacceptable.

The *superego* begins to develop when a child identifies with the same-sexed parent and represses the memories of her former hostility and sexual longing. Along with the sexual identity, the child takes on the shoulds, shouldn'ts, and values of that parent. *Voilà*, the superego!

As the superego matures and gains strength it puts a lot of pressure on the ego to keep the id in line. Some typical examples of superego messages are: "You shouldn't make a mess," "You shouldn't have sex until marriage, and then only to have children," and "You should work hard." Familiar?

The id, the superego, and the ego are constantly interacting with each other—the id saying, "I want," the superego saying, "No!" and the ego trying to figure out how to get what the id wants but in a way that doesn't bother the superego.

Let's take the example of the id wanting to smear feces all over the bathroom because something aroused a feeling of aggression. Immediately the superego says, "No!" but the ego comes up with a compromise: Let the child play in the mud and smear that all over. Thus, the id is satisfied and the superego isn't aware that the mud is a substitute for feces (because if it were there would be hell to pay). This ego-organized compromise is called a *defense mechanism*. It is used not so much to placate the id as to ease the ego's anxiety about the superego's complaints, because anxiety weakens the ego and thereby threatens to allow the id to gain the upper hand.

Obviously, these three—the id, the ego, and the superego—are always struggling for power over each other, and this is how the possibility of neurosis arises. So long as the ego can handle the id without tipping its hand to the superego—and bringing on the superego's wrath with its consequent anxiety—a person can get along fairly well. But if the ego is not strong enough to control the id and negotiate with the superego, then there are problems, because the person's connection to the real world—through the ego—is broken. As Freud said, "When the ego is detached from the reality of the external world, then, under the influence of the internal world, it slips down into psychosis."

Freud also pointed out that one of the ways the ego can become detached from reality is through fantasy. For instance, what the ego perceives as reality is not reality at all, but only what the imagination tells the ego is real. If the person's fantasizing is exaggerated, that could mean big trouble.

Suppose a child in the phallic stage of development perceived his father as hating him (because the father supposedly is jealous of the mother's attention to the child). Every time the father disciplines the boy, the ego, seeing the action through the eyes of the boy's fantasy, would interpret the father's behavior as threatening, hostile, possibly even dangerous. The resulting defense mechanism devised by the ego might be the child's timidity or extreme rebellion. In short, the ego would be overreacting to a threat that doesn't exist except in the imagination of the child.

What Freud is implying is that none of us sees what is real, but only what we think is real, and this is the "reality" to which the ego responds. So, in one sense, we all are neurotic to some degree, depending upon how much our fantasies distort the real world. But a certain amount of neuroticism is tolerable. We become handicapped when, as mentioned before, the ego loses its control of the id.

What you don't know

Can all this intrigue and struggle be going on inside you without your knowledge?

Yes. In a way.

The id, you see, is part of our unconscious mind, so that

we are not aware of its conflicts. The ego and superego are primarily in the conscious mind, but they also have roots extending into the unconscious.

Then why even bother about the unconscious? you may ask, and that's a reasonable question.

The answer is that the conflicts in the unconscious mind express themselves in ways other than through the conscious mind. We may not be aware of our inner struggles as such, but after a while we develop feelings of discomfort and unease—such as an inability to get along with others, a conviction of personal inadequacy, a sense of failure, a pervasive, constant feeling of sorrow. Sometimes we can become physically ill because something in the unconscious is unresolved and unsatisfied, and the tension of that inner conflict is becoming unbearable. In one way or another—perhaps through compulsive behavior, guilt, depression, hysteria—the inner needs will be expressed.

Psychoanalysis, then, is the attempt to remove the ego restraints on the I-wants of the id and allow them to come up into the conscious mind, where we can be aware of them. It is *not*—repeat, *not*—an attempt to give the id permission to do whatever it pleases. I say this because the theory of psychoanalysis often is misinterpreted in that way, and the misunderstanding should not be perpetuated.

Freud believed that once a person knows what is going on inside him, what his needs really are—conflicting though they may be—he can decide for himself which needs should be satisfied and in which way. In others words, he can choose the behavior that best meets his needs yet avoids undesirable consequences.

Obviously, then, psychoanalysis is not for the person who wants a quick solution to his problems. Nor is it for the person who wants to be told what to do to feel better. In psychoanalysis—and even in psychoanalytical therapy—the goal is knowledge of the self, and the application of that knowledge in whichever ways the patient believes are best.

How long does it take? Forever. But let me explain what I mean by forever.

The psychoanalysis or the therapy is complete when the patient is able to analyze his own needs and reconcile them with a fairly objective view of reality. And he continues to do this for the rest of his life. In short, when the patient becomes his own therapist, the formal analysis is ended.

How does it work?

In some very interesting ways.

Theory and therapy

Let's use a hypothetical case to illustrate the difference between psychoanalysis and the psychoanalytic therapy.

Bill is twenty years old and in his second year of college. He isn't doing very well, although he is above average in intelligence. In the beginning of his courses, he got good grades, but he began to dislike his male teachers, and that interfered with his work. Finally the dean of students, a man in late middle age, summons Bill to his office and tells him he just isn't college material and must leave.

Bill is so distraught that he seeks professional help and makes an appointment for a psychoanalytic therapist. During their first interview, Bill explains his feeling that some force inside him is out to destroy him, but he does not know what it is or what to do about it. His therapist tells him to pay particular attention to his dreams, in fact to write them down each morning when he wakes up, and to bring his notes with him to the next session.

The reason the therapist wants Bill to record his dreams is that this is where the id expresses the desires and needs the superego often finds unacceptable. By learning to read Bill's dreams, the therapist can get some idea of what is going on in

Bill's subconscious and perhaps bring the conflict out into the open of the ego.

That night Bill has a dream in which a young boy carrying a walking stick is strolling along a suburban street. Suddenly a man wearing a square cap comes up to the boy, breaks his walking stick, and leaves. The boy then appears in a field among tall white porcelain towers spewing black ink. As the ink runs down around the boy, the man in the square cap appears again and is drowned by the ink.

When Bill wakes up he is understandably shaken. He writes down as much of the dream as he can remember and describes it to his therapist at their next meeting.

Whether the therapist conducts a full psychoanalysis or uses psychoanalytic therapy, her observations and conclusions would be similar, and they would be based upon what Bill says about his problem and his dream. The therapist would note, for instance, that Bill gets into the same predicament with all his male teachers—so perhaps the real problem is in Bill's relationship to his father and is simply spilling over into his schoolwork.

Also, Bill's difficulties are related to performance and achievement, so perhaps Bill interpreted the dean's statement to mean that Bill wasn't man enough to keep up with the other students.

In the dream, the man breaks the boy's walking stick, which the therapist interprets as a little boy's fears of castration during the phallic stage of development. So, she concludes, Bill's problem may be related to some confusion about his sexual identity because of a disturbance during that early time in his life. The fact that Bill is having trouble keeping his grades up is only a symptom of the real problem.

The therapist also notices that Bill is having such a hard time with these unresolved Oedipal issues that he is *regressing* to anal ways of coping with the situation. This is evident in his dream. The ink which drowns the man in the square cap (who could be the dean and/or Bill's father) is a symbol for the feces the unconscious id really would like to use.

If Bill were to undergo a complete psychoanalysis, he would see his therapist three to five times a week for several years. Most of the time Bill would lie on a couch, facing the ceiling, and the therapist would sit behind him, out of sight. Bill would try to say whatever came to his mind, no matter how silly, shocking, or unrelated it might seem. This is called *free association,* and it attempts to coax the unconscious parts of the psyche to express themselves verbally without interference or interpretation by the ego. The object here is to help Bill overcome the ego's defense mechanisms that prevent him from expressing his I-wants directly to his conscious mind.

One of the most important and fascinating events of psychoanalysis is called *transference.* It means that the patient begins to relate to the therapist as he related to his mother or father or some other prominent person in his life. As this happens, the therapist makes the patient aware of (conscious of) his behavior and helps him to uncover his unconscious feelings about that person. Once the patient brings these feelings out into the open, he is able to see the difference between what really caused them and what he imagines to be the cause.

What he does with these differentiations will eventually improve the quality of his life and probably will change his behavior to some degree. But his use of his self-knowledge is not a part, or a goal, of his psychoanalysis.

Now, if Bill were to go to a psychoanalytic therapist, he would see the therapist one or two times a week for several months or about two years. He might sit in a chair facing the therapist, or he might lie on a couch with the therapist behind him, or perhaps sit in a chair turned away from the therapist. Less time would be spent digging into Bill's childhood, looking for the sources of the problem, and transference would not be a major part of the process. Of course, a certain amount of transference would occur, but it would become a subject for analysis only if it interfered with Bill's progress.

Most of the time the therapist would ask Bill questions about the problem that aroused his concern and brought him into therapy. The aim of the questions would be to get Bill to face the true nature of his problem and not just its superficial symptoms. This is not easy and it takes time. Very often there are long periods of silence, during which neither the patient nor the therapist says a word because the patient is resisting the therapist's probing into his subconscious. Sometimes the patient explodes with anger when the therapist gets close to a sore spot in the subconscious. The reason for this is that the subconscious fights very hard to hold on to its secrets, and drawing them out requires very skillful therapy. Ironically, however, when the innermost thoughts and needs are brought into the open, the patient experiences a tremendous feeling of relief. Seeing oneself through the eyes of the ego, rather than through the supercritical squint of the superego, is a real breakthrough. Once the patient becomes aware of his deeper feelings and conflicts, the therapist can discuss different ways in which the patient might satisfy his needs more directly, yet acceptably.

For instance, when Bill feels afraid of his father, he may think of himself as the little boy he was when those fears originated. By going back to those fears he can understand how they might arise in a child—*but* with the therapist's help he now can realize that he is no longer a child. His father does not tower over him. He is fully grown and a man, and he does not have to be afraid of the things that frightened him as a child. If Bill the man can meet up with the fears of the child, he can overcome them. And overcoming them means that he will not have to repeat the kind of behavior that caused his problem.

A matter of options

While psychoanalytic therapy is shorter and directed toward the patient's problems and their solutions, it still is based upon psychoanalytical theory. There is no prescribed way for a patient to change her behavior. The patient must decide that for herself, with the therapist's cooperation, when she is able to differentiate between reality and fantasy. When she is no longer compelled by her blocked needs to behave in the same neurotic ways, she begins to have options, and the options are not the same for all patients.

Here, too, the goal is for the patient to become her own therapist, and for the therapy to go on for the rest of her life.

You could say, actually, that this kind of therapy—or theory—is a *way of life*. And it appears to be a very good way of life for those who can give it the time it requires and put up with the discomfort of their problems during the analytic process.

The amount of time required is one of the drawbacks of either kind of therapy, psychoanalytic therapy requiring an average of two years and psychoanalysis several more than that. Cost is another drawback. A therapy hour in either kind of method costs anywhere from twenty-five to seventy-five dollars, depending upon the therapist and the part of the country in which he practices.

If the prospect of sorting through all the different schools of analytical thought gets you down, take heart. Call your local (city, county, or state) psychiatric association and ask them to explain the different methods of treatment and give you a list of therapists who practice them.

Not everyone with enough time and money can benefit from psychoanalytic therapy or psychoanalysis. Therapists say a person needs a high degree of intelligence, a good education, and especially a well-developed, strong ego—all of which is a pretty stiff entrance requirement.

CHAPTER 9
SEX THERAPY

Bud is on the verge of his second divorce, and the cause is the same. The trouble began when he was a teenager having his first experiences with sex, and he thought he could blame it on youth and inexperience. For a while after his first marriage it seemed to go away, but not for long. Then, between marriages, he had a lot of girls and that didn't help. Neither did a second marriage. And that's a shame, because Bud doesn't want to lose his wife. They seemed to be so right for each other in every other way until—well, when their sex life broke down, everything else seemed to break down too.

Bud's problem is premature ejaculation. He "comes" within seconds after his penis enters the woman's vagina. Usually the woman doesn't have time to experience an orgasm, which makes Bud feel like a sexual failure. His first wife was very demanding, very impatient, and there were nightly arguments. His second wife is more understanding. She wants to help Bud, but he just doesn't know what to do. Rather than repeat the frustrating experience, he has been avoiding sexual contact with his wife. And *that* really caused some problems.

When it comes to sex, Janice and her husband have decided that they must learn to do without it. For Janice, at least, it's too painful, too humiliating. At first, everything is fine. But the moment Janice's husband tries to penetrate her, her vagina closes up like a fist. Janice has no control over it. She's tried everything, even getting slightly drunk, and nothing helps.

Is the problem psychological? Janice's husband thinks it is

and wants her to see a psychiatrist. But that would take such a long time and maybe the problem still wouldn't be solved. Besides, Janice can't bear the possibility that she might have some terrible fear of men in general—or of her husband in particular.

So for the time being Janice and her husband are trying to do without sex. But they're wondering how long that will last. And what will it do to the rest of their relationship?

Mark is thirty-one and has never been married, never had a long-term sexual relationship with a woman. Not that he hasn't wanted to. It's just that he can't. He's impotent. He's been to all kinds of doctors, but no one has been able to help him. And the older he gets, the worse the problem becomes, because each failure is more painful.

Relax, he keeps trying to tell himself, but each time he finds himself sexually attracted to a woman, he gets more and more nervous. He's tired of hoping that "maybe this time it will be different." Because it never is.

To look at Rachel, you would never guess she has a sex problem. Sensuous, lovely, and warm—that's the way you might describe her. And that's the way she is, except in bed. Oh, she enjoys sex, but she just doesn't get as much out of it as she should. Only once or twice has she had an orgasm, and that was so long ago she can hardly remember it.

For three years Rachel has lived with a man she loves. At first she tried to "fake it" when they made love, but that didn't work. Her partner guessed the truth, which was actually a relief. But then he tried harder to give Rachel an orgasm, thinking it was his fault that she couldn't have one, and that made Rachel uncomfortable. Both of them are trying too hard now, and one of these days they're going to admit that they aren't enjoying sex at all anymore. Rachel doesn't even want to think about what will happen then.

The right to sexual happiness

These people have sex problems.

What can they do about them?

Well, there was a time—not many years ago, either—when there wasn't much, if anything, they could do. They certainly couldn't admit their problems, because people didn't talk about sex, not even in the privacy of their homes. And they couldn't do anything about them, because sex itself was considered one big problem everybody just had to put up with as best she could. Fulfillment? Happiness? Enjoyment? Don't be silly!

But the age of sexual permissiveness during the sixties, despite its excesses, changed our sexual expectations. People no longer feel they have to put up with sex problems, and in fact believe they have a right to sexual happiness.

That expressed desire created the atmosphere for sex therapy.

Then came Masters and Johnson with the therapy itself.

In 1954 William Masters and Virginia Johnson (now husband and wife) began their study of sexual dysfunctions in men and women. They believed that the greatest obstacle to the treatment of these problems was massive public and individual ignorance about the physiological and psychological aspects of sex. So for five years they studied every measurable detail of sexual response between men and women—what were the physical symptoms of arousal, what happened during orgasm, what were the stages of arousal and how long did they take? They watched couples make love and measured their blood pressure, respiration, perspiration, pulse, and aftereffects. They watched couples sleep together and found, among other things, that a man and woman sleep closer to each other after intercourse. They recorded their observations and results of their experiments on tape and on film and compiled their conclusions in a best-selling but highly technical book, *Human Sexual Response*. That was followed by *Human Sexual Inadequacy*, another best-seller.

Out of their study they also devised therapeutic techniques to solve the kinds of sexual dysfunctions that were plaguing, and often disrupting, an incredible number of marriages and other man-woman relationships. Their theory was that an unsatisfying sex life could eventually destroy other healthy areas of a marriage. Sex, they concluded, is the highest, most intimate form of communication between a man and a woman, and if a couple can't communicate sexually, then pretty soon they won't even be able to have a meaningful conversation over the breakfast table.

In 1959 in St. Louis, Missouri, Masters and Johnson opened their now-famous clinic for the treatment of sex problems. It goes by the unsexy name of Reproductive Biology Research Foundation and has been the subject of endless sensationalized articles and books about the techniques practiced and taught there. But the truth is, the results have been phenomenal. Men and women from all over the world have come to the clinic to learn how to exercise their right to sexual happiness—and the cure rate is high.

Since the Masters and Johnson therapy was introduced, there have been many others, most of them differing only in slight degrees. So in this chapter we will use the Masters and Johnson procedures as our guide, since they represent most of the other forms of sex therapy now being offered.

Shaping the problem

Men and women can't simply enroll at the sex therapy clinic. They must be referred by a doctor, clergyman, social worker, or other kind of counselor. And in most instances, the person with the problem does not enroll alone—her partner must come along with her and undergo therapy. The reason makes sense: When one partner has a sex problem, the other has a dysfunctional partner, and that also is a problem. So the partner who doesn't have the basic problem is taught how to be helpful to the partner who does. In a sense, it is the marriage or the relationship itself which needs therapy.

No matter what the problem may be, the first few steps of treatment are the same.

The couple enroll for two weeks, just as though they were going on vacation. At the clinic they are received as guests and the accommodations are relaxed and comfortable.

Two therapists, a man and a woman, are assigned to the couple and will meet with them each day for two weeks. During the first day the couple must take a complete physical examination. Then the therapists will take a detailed history of each, the male therapist meeting with the man and the female with the woman. On the second day another history is taken, but this time the therapists switch—the male therapist takes the woman's history and the female the man's. In this way the therapists can check for any omitted details and also can determine whether either partner is more comfortable with someone of his own or the opposite sex.

On the third day the couple and the therapists sit down for a "round table" discussion which begins with the therapists offering their findings about the cause of the problem and the route to its solution. The couple are encouraged to ask questions and, if they have any objections to the findings, to refute them. When everyone is in agreement, the actual treatment begins.

The first thing the couple learn to do is to enjoy their own and each other's bodies, something which sex therapists tell us many people do not know how to do. The procedure is called *sensate focus*, and it means learning to experience and communicate pleasure. On the first day the couple are told to spend two short periods of time alone together, without their therapists, taking turns touching each other's body and telling each other what feels good and what doesn't. They must avoid the genital areas and the woman's breasts, and must not attempt intercourse. This technique is especially helpful for the impotent man and nonorgasmic woman because the pressure is off: They don't have to worry about how well they will perform and react because all they have to do is enjoy the experience.

As each partner gives the other directions—higher, lower, faster, lighter, etc.—the couple begin to discover how many areas of the body are sensually responsive.

Once the couple have learned to experience and communicate pleasure, they are ready to go on to genital stimulation. But, again, no intercourse. The goal here is for each one to enjoy his own bodily sensations without the pressure to perform.

Specific solutions

Now the treatment begins to vary, depending upon the kind of problem it is attempting to solve.

Bud, you remember, was a premature ejaculator and will be given the *squeeze technique*. This means that his wife will be taught how to hold and squeeze the tip of the penis at the moment when Bud tells her he is about to come—which may seem like a terrible thing for her to do, but really isn't. It does, however, require complete cooperation and communication between the partners.

When they are alone together, they do their "homework." Bud's wife begins by stimulating him manually until they master the squeeze technique (which, incidentally, does not hurt). Then, with Bud lying on his back and his wife on top, his wife inserts his penis into her vagina—taking some of the responsibility upon herself and off Bud. Bud then begins to thrust until he is near the point of no return. That is when he signals his wife, who lifts herself off his penis and squeezes the tip in the way she was taught to do, delaying his ejaculation. They repeat this procedure for fifteen or twenty minutes, or as much longer as they like, and finally Bud is allowed to come. Eventually Bud will be able to hold off ejaculation for longer and longer periods, until the problem no longer exists. (The cure rate is 97.8 percent.)

Vaginismus

Janice's problem is relatively simple to treat and the cure rate is 100 percent.

The most important obstacle for the therapists to overcome is the conviction of the couple that Janice's condition is psychological rather than physical, and that it is somehow indicative of hidden hostility toward her husband. So the first specific treatment step is another physical examination of Janice, with her husband present. Physically it is an uncomfortable experience for Janice, but when the examining gynecologist is able to demonstrate how her vaginal muscles contract involuntarily, Janice is greatly relieved. The problem, obviously, is physical.

For the next several days Janice will insert a dilator—a rod of metal or plastic—into her vagina. She will begin with a small one and gradually increase the size, leaving it in place for several hours at a time. When the larger dilators can be inserted comfortably, Janice and her husband will attempt intercourse, which usually will be successful. For the next several weeks Janice will use the dilator for a few minutes before intercourse and after that probably will not need it again.

Along with this physical therapy there is daily psychological counseling to help Janice release her resentment and hostility toward her husband. Part of any good sex therapy is a lesson in direct communication between husband and wife.

Impotence

Mark's problem is somewhat special. Not that impotence is that serious, but it has kept him from having a sexual relationship with a woman, and therefore he does not have a partner.

So, in this unusual instance, Mark is enrolled alone and is provided with a surrogate partner. She is a carefully chosen and trained woman who can give Mark the psychological as well as the physiological support he will need during treatment.

Mark and his partner will get to know each other over dinner and conversation the first evening. Of course he will feel awkward in the beginning, but after a few hours in the company of a relaxed, compassionate woman he will begin to think of her as a friend.

Mark and his partner will go through the same sensate focus exercises as any other couple. Then, as the treatment becomes specialized, Mark's partner will use several ways to stimulate his penis until he gets an erection. Then, as in the treatment for premature ejaculation, Mark will lie on his back and his partner will take the upper position. She will insert his penis into her vagina, relieving him of some of the pressure to perform, because it is this pressure that intensifies impotence. She also is the one who will do most of the moving, encouraging Mark to relax, enjoy—and eventually to have a complete and perfectly joyous sexual experience. As this procedure is repeated, Mark will gain confidence in his ability to come—and that is the end of his problem. (The cure rate varies: For primary impotence, which means the man never had an orgasm, it is 59.4 percent; for secondary impotence—only an occasional orgasm—it is 73.8 percent.)

The nonorgasmic woman

Rachel needs to be given a sense of control and so she will be the one on top, with her partner lying on his back. Sex therapists believe that women have been pinned down under men for too long and that this may be one cause for an inability to have orgasms.

Incidentally, you will notice the absence of the word *frigid* here. That's because sex therapists consider the word not only demeaning but inaccurate. A woman who cannot experience orgasm is not cold or frozen or unresponsive in any way. She simply has not experienced an orgasm. But she almost certainly can.

As instructed, after Rachel inserts her partner's penis into her vagina, she lies still, allowing herself to enjoy the pleasant sensations that accompany penetration. There is no demand for her to have an orgasm. She is not even to try. Enjoyment is her only goal.

On successive days Rachel may begin to thrust a little. So will her partner. But Rachel can stop or ask her partner to stop at any time. She is always in control. Gradually she will thrust more, and so will he. Sometimes they may stop to caress and then resume thrusting. And gradually, as Rachel becomes caught up in the sensual pleasures of intercourse, she will have an orgasm—in her own time and in her own way. (The cure rate here is 80.7 percent.)

A matter of position

You have probably noticed that in each one of these examples the woman is on top during intercourse. It's not a coincidence. What is called a *lateral coital position* is recommended by sex therapists for all couples, because, for one thing, it is very comfortable, and, for another, it provides the best physical opportunities for experimentation. And, as we've seen in Mark's case, it also helps to control the man's ejaculation, should that be needed.

Who can be helped?

Sex therapy techniques are most effective when the sex problem is specific, such as the examples we have described.

The results are not as dramatic when neurotic attitudes—such as spite, guilt, retaliation, and self-destructiveness—underlie the sexual dysfunction.

But the most important necessity for a cure is the overall relationship of the couple. If the marriage or the living arrangement of two people is sound, if there is mutual respect and healthy love, then the chances for solving a sex problem are excellent.

So if you aren't getting the most out of your sex life, do something about it! Remember, you—like everyone else—have a right to sexual happiness.

CHAPTER 10 TRANSACTIONAL ANALYSIS

Do you ever wonder why you behave differently with some people than with others? Of course, you may know some better than others and be more relaxed in their company. But that isn't the only reason why you feel free to have more fun with some people and not as much with others.

Do you ever wonder why certain people annoy you, yet you can't put your finger on a reason for it?

And why is it that you're able to handle some situations in a perfectly mature way, while others make you feel like a frightened child?

Why can't you just be yourself, all the time?

Yourself, Inc.

The reason is that your conscious mind is composed of many different parts. And they don't always respond at the same time or to the same things.

Other people are the same way.

So, when two or more people interact, it may be only a specific part of each person's consciousness that is responding to the other. Not the whole person. Only part. Or parts.

You—and the other person—are like giant corporations with many subdivisions, each one doing its own thing in its own way.

A tribute to Eric Berne

During the fifties, psychiatrist Eric Berne became deeply interested in these specific parts of the human personality. In his group therapy work Berne noticed that his patients would respond in different ways to each other, and not always in the same way to the same person. Sometimes they behaved as their parents might have behaved, admonishing or advising a child. Sometimes they were more like the child they might have been. And sometimes they behaved in a perfectly rational, unemotional adult manner.

Berne tossed out the usual technical jargon and called these three basic parts of the conscious mind the *Parent, Adult,* and *Child.* He described them as three possible ego states—roughly corresponding to the superego, ego, and id of psychoanalytic therapy—which could motivate the way we interact with others. This interaction he called a *transaction,* which actually is an encounter between two or more persons. Then Berne came up with a system of analyzing these transactions—and there you have transactional analysis, or TA, as it is popularly called. It means you can tell when you and another person are in the Parent, Adult, or Child ego state as you interact with each other. You can also learn to change your ego state to suit a particular situation or person.

It can help anyone

TA, its practitioners point out, is something anyone can learn. You don't have to be sick or have a specific problem, although it definitely is a problem-oriented therapy. But, according to Thomas A. Harris, author of *I'm OK—You're OK* and a disciple of Berne's, it can help anyone to live a fuller, more enjoyable life.

Learning to analyze the transactions between your Parent, Adult, and Child and those of another person, or persons, is a major part of the therapy. As you learn how these ego states fluctuate in response to the stimulus of the other person, you begin to understand why your behavior sometimes gets a bit out of control, and what you can do to change it.

We are talking about the conscious mind here. TA does not deal with concepts of the subconscious mind except as it influences and expresses itself in the conscious mind, so it is a much quicker examination of the personality than is psychoanalysis. Most of the time TA is done in groups no larger than eight, although occasionally a person may begin by seeing the therapist on an individual basis. The meetings last for two hours. Sometimes the length of attendance is ten group meetings, but more often there is no set time limit. Most groups are ongoing, with new members coming in whenever there is an opening—meaning a member has left. A member leaves when he feels he has solved his conflict or problem.

One of Berne's most valuable contributions was the language of TA, which is popular to the point of being outright slang. It makes the analysis pleasant, often fun, and easy to understand. Learning this language is an important part of the therapy itself.

An introduction to your PAC

Let's assume you are enrolling in a TA group. You don't have a specific problem. You just have occasional discomfort about the inconsistency of your behavior.

You have some interesting things to learn . . .

First, in an introductory lecture you will be introduced to the three basic parts of your consciousness: your Adult, your Parent, and your Child. They will become evident as demonstrators—and finally you and other members—play roles in situations typical of everyday life: transactions between husband and wife, teacher and student, parent and child, employer and employee.

But how did you get that way?

Well, your Child came with you into the world when you were born. Then your Parent began to take shape. And then your Adult. All of them in rapid succession, but each of them with a totally different response to the world around you.

Eric Berne, who began his career as a trained Freudian psychoanalyst, believed that the human mind records and retains everything that has happened to the person. So, however you thought when you were a child, whatever you feared, desired, smelled, heard, saw, and felt, is still there in you, even though now you are grown. This collection of childhood experiences and sensitivity, this "cassette" which can be played back whenever something in the present reminds us—consciously or unconsciously—of something that happened in those early days, we call the Child, or C for short.

But there is your *OK Child* and your *Not-OK Child*. Your OK Child is pleasure-loving, adventuresome, and spontaneous. It loves and hates without inhibition. It laughs, despairs, and cries. It is the source of your creativity and imagination. Actually a very pleasant fellow, and the most natural part of you.

The Not-OK Child did whatever it had to do—or thought it had to do—to get the parents' love and approval, so don't expect it to be spontaneous. It learned to inhibit its own wishes and needs in favor of those the parents found more desirable. For instance, it may have learned to play helpless, act sad, or be unusually competent, according to what it sensed its parents wanted it to be. It is called Not-OK because that is the way it always felt when it was doing something its parents didn't like. And out of this Not-OKness, it conformed.

Your Parent was born out of your close association with your parents. I'm sure you, like everyone else, can remember your mother and father saying, "Don't do this, don't do that, watch out for such and such, always remember such and such, be sure to do this or that." They rarely told you why, and if they did, the reason probably didn't make sense to you anyway. Now all those shoulds and shouldn'ts are there in your recordlike mind, and they can be played back at any time. When that happens, you are *coming on Parent*, in TA language.

As with the Child, your Parent also is divided into OK

Parent and *Not-OK Parent.* When you come to a crosswalk and remember to look both ways before stepping into the street, that is your OK Parent looking out for the safety of the OK Child. Or you are at the kitchen table, chatting with a friend and finishing a cup of coffee, and suddenly you tell yourself, "I should put the cream back in the refrigerator before it sours." That is your OK Parent sending you a message. It wants you to grow and learn to master life.

Then there is the Not-OK Parent, who is out to stifle the OK Child and reinforce the negative feelings in the Not-OK Child. When you feel something criticizing you, telling you not to do something that really might be fun, or telling you in no uncertain terms that you'll never amount to much, that's your Not-OK Parent.

Suppose you're at a party and you've had a few drinks. You're having a good time but you decide not to drink any more because you know you have to drive home. That was your OK Parent giving you a life-supporting message: "You shouldn't drink too much if you have to drive home by yourself." No quarrel with that.

But now the music is playing and you're standing off to one side just dying to move to the rhythm. A good-looking person you've been eyeing all evening walks up to you and says, "Hey, let's dance." And what do you do? You shake your head and say, "No, I'm fine right here."

Now you and I happen to know that you would like nothing more than to move out and dance until you can't stand up. Especially with that person. So what stopped you? Why couldn't your natural OK Child, who loves to have fun, say yes to the invitation? The answer is that your Not-OK Parent came on strong with something like: "If you go out on that dance floor and make a fool of yourself everyone will laugh at you." The original killjoy.

The third part of your consciousness is your Adult, which

came into being when you were about ten months old and beginning to move around. With the power of locomotion came the ability to question life for yourself, and this is primarily what the Adult does. It is not emotional. It works strictly on the facts. It processes information coming in from all around you and makes decisions based on its evaluations of this data. Most important, it also evaluates the data fed into it by your Child and your Parent. If, for example, the Child wants to dash across the street and the Parent says, "No, there might be a car coming and you could get hurt," the Adult will look up and down the street, observe that there is a lot of traffic, and decide that the Parent's information is valid. No, you won't dash across the street—you'll wait for the traffic to stop and then you'll walk to the other side in perfect safety.

If, however, the Parent tells the Child, "Don't cross the street—you'll get run over!" the Adult in time will see that others can cross the street safely if they look both ways and obey the traffic signals. In that case the Adult will conclude that the Parent's advice is invalid and will cancel it out (ignore it). That is, *if* the Adult is doing the thinking and deciding—and it isn't always.

Who's making up your mind?

Reality. That's a loaded word, but we all have to deal with it. Trouble is, no two people see it the same way. And, according to transactional analysts, no one person sees it the same way all the time. It depends upon which ego state we are in.

An ego state is the way we feel at a particular moment, and for our purposes here it means: Are we feeling Parent, Adult, or Child? Because how we feel will determine how we see reality and how we behave in response to our perception. For instance, if we are feeling Adult, we will be able to make decisions quickly and unemotionally and will go about our business in a logical, competent manner. Our behavior is consistent with our ego state. But suppose the Child or the Parent intrudes while we are in an Adult ego state and causes us to behave in a childlike manner? Then our behavior is called *discrepant,* because it doesn't match our ego state.

Let's say you are at the beach turning somersaults on the sand (OK Child). You stop and look at your watch (Adult) and decide you should be getting ready to leave soon (OK Parent). Nothing wrong with that, is there? That's because the intrusions were helpful messages from other parts of your consciousness.

But suppose you are driving past the beach on your way to a business appointment (Adult). It's a beautiful day and the sun is hot on your arms and you wish you could go for a swim (OK Child). So you park your car, get into your suit, and to hell with your appointment! (Also OK Child.) But after your swim you feel guilty (Not-OK Parent) and call your business appointment and tell him your car broke down (Not-OK Child).

In the first example, you recognized the intrusions and were able to control them. In the second example you were completely unaware of your changing ego states and they were in charge.

When you were at the beach having a good time, your Adult was able to control the intrusions of the other ego states, and your decision was consistent with an Adult view of reality. But when you abandoned your business appointment in favor of a swim, your Child took over from your Adult, imposing its child's-eye view of reality on you, causing you to make an irrational decision. That is called *contaminating the Adult,* and it can cause a lot of trouble. Fortunately, there also is a way to *decontaminate your Adult.*

As you learn to recognize each of your three ego states you will sense which one is in control at a given moment. For instance, if you are on your way to a business appointment and pass by a lovely beach, you may very well feel a strong desire to go for a swim and forget about your obligations. But then you will acknowledge the intrusion of the OK Child:

Of course it would be delightful to have a swim, you'll agree from your Adult ego state. *However, you have a previous engagement. As soon as you have a free afternoon, you'll take that swim.* In that way you let the OK Child know it has a right to enjoy life, yet you prevent the intrusion (and confusion) of the Not-OK Parent and the Not-OK Child. And you feel perfectly comfortable. That's how decontamination works.

Transacting with others

Whenever you interact with another person, you do it through one of your ego states. In other words, you come on Parent, Adult, or Child in what you say or do. And in doing so, you are addressing yourself (or, rather, your ego state) to one of the other person's ego states. For instance:

Student to roommate:

"It's getting hot in here. Should we turn on the air conditioner?" (Adult to Adult, processing data for making a decision.)

Or:

"How can you stand the heat in here? Do I always have to be the one to turn on the air conditioner?" (Parent to Child, a critical putdown.)

Or:

"I'm so hot! Can't we turn on the air conditioner?" (Child to Parent, complaining, seeking help.)

Any number of combinations are possible and any number may be successful, provided the other person responds in the expected manner and from the anticipated ego state.

For instance, in the first example, the anticipated transaction would be:

"Yes, it is hot. I'm all for a little air conditioning."

That would be a complementary transaction, meaning that

the ego state (Adult, in this instance) aimed at is the one that responds.

But suppose the reply were something like this:

"You're always hot! You ought to live in Alaska!"

That's a crossed transaction, meaning that an unanticipated ego state responded (in this instance, the Parent talking to the Not-OK Child). The transaction failed, and very likely the two people involved retreated into silence and confusion.

We could go on with many other examples, but I'm sure you have already thought of several from your own experience.

Pushing the right button

In your TA sessions, as you and the other members of the group role-play, you will not only begin to see your own ego states in action, but you will begin to learn how to move from one state to another to avoid or to deal with such things as crossed transactions. For instance, if you are aiming at the other person's Adult ego state, but she responds from her Not-OK Child, you can then come on OK Parent and reassure the Not-OK Child. From that point, you both may be able to go on to the Adult ego state and have a satisfactory transaction.

With all this emphasis on the Adult ego state, you may get the idea that you are supposed to try to behave as an Adult all the time. Not so. The Parent has its place in your life, and so does your Child. You can't have any fun in life, nor can you be creative, without giving way to your OK Child, and you can use your Parent in many practical, helpful ways (such as reminding you to turn off the lights when you leave a room and thereby save energy, or to fill up your gas tank before taking a long trip).

What's your game?

Any description of transactional analysis would be incomplete without a reference to Eric Berne's best-seller, *Games*

People Play. This was the book that made TA part of our everyday language by showing us how our Parent, Adult, and Child interact with the Parent, Adult, and Child of others.

A *game* is something all of us play, although all of us do not play in the same way. We play different kinds of games and assume different kinds of roles in the games.

Games begin with something called *strokes*, which is Berne's label for the attention every human being must get in one way or another. Without attention—without strokes—we would die (and this has been confirmed by the death of infants in foundling homes who were given every other form of life-sustaining nourishment *except* attention). And if we can't get enough positive strokes, such as kisses, hugs, smiles, praise, caresses, we will settle for the negative ones, such as frowns, slaps, rebukes, criticism. All of this, of course, is quite unconscious, as is the way in which our parents dispense their strokes. However, parents do dispense strokes selectively, according to the way they want the child to behave, and the child will do whatever he must in order to get the desired attention and approval.

Can you see what is happening?

The child's behavior patterns are being shaped by the strokes he receives. This shaping is what Berne calls the person's *life script*, because it definitely dictates the role the person will play for the rest of his life—unless he realizes what is going on and learns how to change his script according to his own desires.

As in so many things in TA, there are good games and bad games, life-loving games and life-defeating games, and herein lies the difference between a fulfilled life and a frustrated one. For instance, if a parent, through his dispensation of strokes, communicates to a child that she is to be a roaring success, then the child may attempt to manipulate others into awarding her that success. That may, of course, mean that the child develops and exercises her talents in such a way that success is the natural outcome of her efforts. Perhaps she is the kind of person who says to herself, "I can write better than Shakespeare could!" and ultimately proves that to be quite true—or almost. Fine. That's a life-loving game.

But another child with a success script may try getting to the top by stepping on everyone in his path, hoping to make himself look good by making others look bad. And that's a life-defeating game in which everyone gets hurt.

Games, in short, are transactions with an ulterior motive, which Berne labels a *gimmick*. The persons playing the game may appear to be doing one thing while they really want—and will attempt to get—something quite different. The gimmick, however, must always conform to the person's life script.

WDY . . . YB

The most common game in groups of all kinds—social, business, or family—is called *Why Don't You . . . Yes, But*, or WDY . . . YB. I'm sure you will recognize it as it is acted out in your TA course something like this:

Eileen is a woman in her early forties, attractive, outspoken, vivacious. She begins by telling the others in the group that she has a problem: She wants to get a job and get back into the world now that her children are grown, but her skills are out of date.

Immediately someone in the group comes to her rescue. "*Why don't you* take a refresher course in shorthand and typing?" Lou suggests.

"*Yes, but* I don't know where there are such courses," Eileen says.

"*Why don't you* call up your local colleges and ask them?" Lou says.

"*Yes, but* if I did take such a course, I'm not sure I'd really want to get back into that kind of work."

"*Why don't you* look for something else?" says Lou.

"Yes, *but* where would I look?"

And so on and on, until Lou is exhausted and someone else takes over the suggestions. Eileen, meanwhile, looks happier and happier. Why? Because she is getting her strokes and confirming her life script.

Here's how it works:

WDY . . . YB, like any other game, is played on two levels. On the surface it looks as if one adult is describing a problem she wants to solve and the others are offering solutions. The transaction appears to be between each person's Adult ego state: "I have a problem" being the stimulus and "Maybe I can help" being the response.

But look again! And this time look a little deeper.

On the second level, Eileen is presenting herself as a helpless Child and Lou is coming on Parent. No matter how many times Eileen implies that she cannot be helped, Lou still comes to the rescue, which is exactly what Eileen wants. And both of them are getting their strokes: Eileen with a life script as the helpless Child, and Lou playing his prescribed role as responsible Parent. On both sides this is an unconscious transaction. Consciously, and on the social level, both believe they are behaving as Adults.

This game could go on forever, and in some people's lives it does. But if Eileen or Lou suddenly switched to the role of Adult on the deeper level of their game, the game could no longer be played. If, for example, Lou were to say to Eileen, "Listen, I've given you all kinds of suggestions and you've rejected every one of them. I don't see any sense in continuing this way," Eileen would become confused. She would either have to respond as an Adult to Lou's Adult, and solve her problem, in which case there would be no more reason to play the game, or she would withdraw and continue as a Child, but all by herself, and there would be no gimmick to confirm her life script.

In your TA sessions, as you are introduced to the many games people can and do play in their interactions, you will begin to spot your own little maneuvers. And here is where you can actually change your behavior. Even deep-seated problems, such as fear of authority figures, compulsive drinking or eating, underachievement, insecurity, fear of intimacy, can be analyzed and solved through use of the appropriate ego state.

Getting your act together

Learning to analyze your transactions does not mean that you become as sober as a judge in everything you do. Uh-uh. It does mean that you can choose the kind of behavior that suits a particular situation and achieve what you need.

Yes, you can have more fun with some people than with others. But it is important to know when and with whom. You don't want your Child making these decisions for you, which may be what is happening in your life right now. After all, your Child may want to have fun with the chairman of the board, and that probably isn't a good idea.

When you can recognize your Parent, Adult, and Child ego states, you can choose which one is best suited to handle the situation. And it is your Adult who should do the choosing, *always*. So let your Adult deal with the chairman of the board, but perhaps your Child is the one to dictate your behavior at a picnic, where all you want to do is have fun. As for your Parent, well, how about letting your Parent plan what you're going to have for dinner tonight.

A note about cost: It's hard to estimate exactly how much the entire process will cost but it's in the same price range as any one of the group therapies.

CHAPTER 11 GROWTH TECHNIQUES

For five years Gail has been assistant to the sales manager, who has often said he couldn't do without her. Now the sales manager is leaving and the company is looking for someone to replace him. Gail would love to get the job and she knows she could handle it. But everyone seems to assume that a sales manager ought to be a man, and Gail can't get up enough nerve to suggest that a woman could do the job just as well. She knows she ought to see the company president and tell him she wants to be considered a candidate—but every time she approaches his office she can't bring herself to knock on the door.

Oh well, she's not doing too badly where she is.

Or is she?

Claude wishes he could quite smoking. It's getting in his way. He's an actor, and when he plays a role that doesn't allow him to smoke, he can't get his mind off cigarettes. He's tried to stop the habit so many times, but he always ends up ill-tempered and jumpy, which is worse than smoking so far as he's concerned. It isn't only the cigarettes that are getting Claude down. He just isn't able to project himself into his roles as well as he did. He'd like to be more creative, more productive, maybe even direct someday.

But maybe this edginess will pass.

And maybe it won't.

An adman's life is hectic, but Jeff used to be able to take it a lot better. Lately he feels tired all the time, no matter how much sleep he gets. He had a complete physical recently and everything was okay. Still, he can see that his muscles are sagging, and he can't walk up one flight of stairs without huffing and puffing. The way he feels is affecting his work, too, and that worries him. He finds it hard to concentrate, and the new ideas aren't coming quickly enough these days.

Yeah, well, maybe it's middle age and he'll just have to accept it.

But why should he?

If I can only get through the rest of this year I'll be all right, Paula keeps telling herself. She's a senior now and soon she'll have her degree. Then all the nights of study will be over—all the missed meals and the cramming of information into a mind that wants more time to reflect will give way to a lovely, serene routine. Funny, her vision of her future is as vague as that—a lovely, serene routine. She doesn't know what she wants to do for a living, or where she wants to live, or how she might contribute something worthwhile to life on earth. In those rare moments when she is perfectly frank with herself, she has to admit she simply doesn't care. She doesn't seem to have a sense of direction or any particular desires to fulfill. In other words, she's depressed. That's why she gets so many headaches lately. Life simply has no zest right now.

Later, maybe, things will be different.

But does she really think so?

These people aren't handicapped. They are getting along all right in life, and they probably could go on in the same way indefinitely. But you certainly couldn't say that they're getting as much out of life as they should.

Continued pressure is wearing them down. Some of them are stagnating because they have used up all the resources they think they have, and now life is a matter of repetition rather than renewal. The challenge has been met and overcome—and so what else is new? Either you run too fast or you start winding down. And maybe your expectations were just too great to begin with, right?

No.

Life doesn't have to be that way.

In fact, life *isn't* that way. The challenges should be greater, not fewer, and the rewards should be more satisfying as you discover more of yourself.

Ah! That's just it! How much of yourself have you really discovered? Are you sure there isn't more? *Much* more? Are there perhaps some talents you haven't tapped, haven't even realized? Are you using your mind as well as it was meant to be used? Are you still growing?

Yes, I said *growing*. And by that I mean becoming more of what you really are. Because if you aren't growing, then you can't possibly be satisfied with your life. There are areas of yourself that are crying out for expression.

If you have that vague sense of "something beyond" that you can't quite define, something that seems to say *You can be more than you are*, pay attention to it. Don't toss it away as wishful thinking. That restlessness, that down-in-the-dumps feeling is a message to you from yourself: Explore. Find. Use. Be. Grow. And continue to explore. One of the growth techniques may be exactly what you need.

They are called techniques rather than therapies because they do not attempt to solve major problems, although they can be used in combination with therapies to help people attain the means to survive. More often, though, these techniques are used to prevent the onset of major problems that can arise from long periods of anxiety and depression. But the most valuable contribution of the growth techniques is to put people in touch with their own vast potential for physical, psychological, and spiritual well-being.

How do they work? In several different ways, although you also will find some similarities. Almost all of them will teach you how to relax. Some will stress physical exercise and development, some will lead you to mental processes you never knew existed, some will teach you to play roles and visualize, and some will use combinations of several methods.

Mainly, they are for people who want to get more out of life.

CHAPTER 12 ARICA TRAINING

When Oscar Ichazo was a very young man, he did what many of us wish we could do: He traveled all over the world trying to find the meaning of life. He left the shelter of his wealthy Chilean family and worked at anything he could get in order to study with Zen monks, Sufi masters, Tibetan lamas, Jesuit priests, and even experts in Japanese martial arts. Then, after plunging into every religion and cult he could find, he put them aside and consulted the depths of his own mind. All the schools of thought he had investigated seemed to be different only on the surface. At the core of each one was the same statement: *Life has meaning if you will believe.*

Well, that was too much mysticism for Oscar. Perhaps in another time, long ago, faith alone would have been the answer, he decided. But not today. Not in our technological world. Contemporary men and women need something practical. They need science.

And that's when Arica was born. It is named for the Chilean town where Oscar's family lived, to which he returned to open a small school. In a precise and "scientific" manner, he began to teach others what he had learned—and then some. That was in 1971. Now Arica has headquarters in New York City and centers in cities all over the world.

If you are stable

If you want to stop drinking or find out why you hate your mother, then don't go to Arica. It is not a therapy, and any Arica trainer will tell you that. Arica is an educational experience intended to enhance your life, not solve your problems. If you want to become more aware of your inner resources, if you want to deepen your relationships and find your place in society, then Arica will be happy to accept you as a student. Note that word *student*. Not *patient*.

If you have climbed to the top of your mountain and feel pretty blah about it, then Arica would like to stimulate you. If you are benumbed by the stresses of your life, then Arica would like to put you in touch with your inner source of energy. The reason you aren't getting all you should out of life, Aricans claim, is that you are projecting your negativism onto everything you see, hear, touch, smell, and taste. Plus everything you think, imagine, and do. What you call reality isn't that at all. It is only a reflection of your inner shadows.

But you can change all that.

You see, the real you—that inner self—is an optimistic person who radiates energy, wisdom, charm, persuasion, joy, love, and beauty. And that self should project itself onto your whole environment so that reality becomes as glowing as your inner being. But your inner radiation is blocked by all the negative experiences in your past, which in turn color the world around you. So if the world looks gray to you, it's you who make it look that way.

Arica training insists that you accept responsibility for the way you are. But you must also accept the possibility of change.

An à la carte curriculum

So the purpose of Arica training is to make you aware of that positive inner self and remove the negative blocks to its expression. It is done through a series of exercises designed to develop every facet of your being: body, emotions, mind, and spirit.

The most comprehensive Arica training is a forty-day residency, during which you will be taught how to meditate, how to relax your body and move it in ways that relieve tension, how to gaze upon colorful yantras (geometric designs) and contemplate. You will chant phrases and repeat Sanskrit sounds (called mantras) which will help you shut out the distractions of your anxious concerns and pay more attention to your inner voice; you will sing, you will dance, and you will learn some very pleasant exercises based on breathing rather than muscular exertion. You also will participate in some encounter-type reviews of your past life, not for the sake of analyzing it, but rather to understand it and put it to rest.

There are four hundred exercises in all, and most of them will be done in a group setting.

A very important part of Arica training is a high-protein diet, enriched with a drink called Dragon's Milk, to help you maintain the high level of energy you will experience as your course progresses.

Focus on you

The goal of Arica training is "to develop consciousness to the point where graduates experience increased happiness in their daily lives, greater vitality and energy, the replacement of negative emotional states by positive ones, greater efficiency in work, increased ability to make decisions, a greater sense of unity within, a reduction of useless mental chatter, and improved relations with family, friends and work associates."

Some critics, however, feel that Arica places too much emphasis on the intellect and not enough on discovering the source of one's anxiety or boredom. They also point to the many Arica students who fare well only while they are in close contact with other Aricans, yet seem to regain their negative attitudes after they are on their own.

Criticism has also been aimed at the Arica stores which are part of every center and sell such accessories as brightly colored hooded robes for meditating, geometrically designed yantras to hang on a wall, and the high-protein Dragon's Milk. None of the articles are cheap. But Arica officials remind us that they are a nonprofit organization, and whatever is earned in the stores goes back into the training of more Aricans.

CHAPTER 13
ASSERTIVENESS TRAINING

It happened again. Your next-door neighbor caught you just as you were getting in your car and asked if you would mind stopping at the post office and mailing a package for her. And you do mind. Very much. Because you're in a hurry and you won't be going anywhere near the post office. Besides, your neighbor does this almost every time you walk out the door. You'd like to say no. You'd also like to tell her to run her own errands for a change. But do you? You do not. No. Instead, you smile somewhat weakly and hold out your hand for the package—which turns out to be rather large and poorly wrapped. You know you'll have to buy some tape and string and do a better packaging job or the post office won't accept it. Which, of course, is what you will do.

In the meantime, while you're playing Goody Two-Shoes, you're actually smoldering with repressed rage. Before you know it, you'll let it out on someone who doesn't deserve it. Or maybe you'll keep it inside you, where it will surely turn into an ache of some sort, which you don't deserve.

Oh well, you tell yourself, that's just your nature. You're such a good sport, people take advantage of you. But what can you do about it? You were born that way.

You can't stand the way the guy in the office down the hall keeps asking you out to lunch—"to talk over some business matters"—and then sticks you with the bill. Sure, your expense account covers it, but why should your department bear the cost of the new guy's education? Why can't he buy your lunch? Or, better yet, why can't you each pay for your own lunch out of your own pockets?

You were going to suggest that to him the last time. You had your mind all made up and your speech all worked out. But when the waiter came with the bill, and your friend looked away, you reached for it. And you paid for it. And you'll be the one called on the carpet by the accounting department when they start wondering why the two of you can't discuss business matters in your office and save those expensive lunches for your clients.

But what can you do? You're a soft touch. It's your nature.

Know your rights

If you fit into either of the above categories, or into one of the many similar situations most of us fit into, I have news for you: You weren't born to be a patsy. No one was or is. If you don't believe me, ask an assertiveness training therapist. He'll tell you that you have as many rights as the next person, and that you ought to learn how to stand up for them.

You don't have to do things you don't want to do.

You don't have to say yes when you really want to say no.

You don't have to make excuses—or even give a reason—when you say no.

If you don't like the way someone behaves toward you, you can say so, right to the person's face and in so many words.

If you feel resentful, hurt, or angry, you can tell the person who is making you feel that way.

And you can do all these things without hurting anyone. In other words, you can stand up for your own rights without stepping on somebody's toes.

It's called *asserting yourself*. It means you stop being a patsy. It means you recognize your right not to be such a good sport or a soft touch all the time. Finally, you realize that you have a right to maintain your dignity and self-respect, and that you are the only one who can safeguard that right.

No, you can't snap your fingers and become an instant assertive person. It takes training and it takes time. But the rewards can make a big difference in your life.

One step at a time

Assertiveness training grew out of behavior modification techniques, and is similar to BT in that it seeks to change the way a person responds to her environmental stimuli. If you can't stand up for your rights, that's because you learned to back down. So now you can unlearn the old habits and learn some new ones.

But AT, as assertiveness training is called for short, goes beyond BT. It not only reduces the anxiety you feel because you can't assert yourself, but also teaches you the kind of social skills you will need to be assertive.

AT is not a problem-oriented technique. If you want to get over stage fright or phobias, BT is the therapy to try. AT is for people who don't know how to make the most of themselves.

One thing must be made clear: Being assertive is *not* the same as being aggressive. When you assert yourself you simply ask for what is yours without depriving anyone else of a thing. When you're aggressive, you get what you want at the expense of the other person. And although we are emphasizing non-assertiveness as the behavior to be changed here, AT is also for aggressive people who would like to become less so.

You can take your training on an individual basis with your therapist if you want to, but during recent years group work has been found to be more effective. It also is less expensive. So let's assume that you have just joined a group.

You will meet once a week for an hour and a half or three hours, and for as long as ten months in some instances. There will be at least two and possibly as many as four therapists present at each meeting, because the therapists' work is extremely demanding. The cost will vary, depending on how long the therapy takes and where you go for help.

Before your first group meeting you will have an interview with one of your therapists and you will fill out a detailed questionnaire which will give the therapist an idea of the extent of your inability to assert yourself in many different kinds of situations. And don't worry. This is not an encounter type of group meeting where you will be urged to assert yourself in extremely difficult situations. Quite the contrary: You will take things one step at a time, perhaps beginning with an assignment to dial Information and ask the operator for a number. You see, the goal here is to keep your anxiety level down at all times so that you can begin to associate assertion with a comfortable feeling.

Gradually, as in behavior therapy, you will move on to assignments which would ordinarily cause you more anxiety, but by this time you will have had a number of successful experiences and plenty of group support for your efforts. Perhaps you will have boarded a bus and asked for change of a five-dollar bill. You will have bought something you didn't want and returned the merchandise for a refund. You will have asked directions from a passing stranger.

What to say, and how

So far this sounds like BT, doesn't it? Well, so far it is. But now you will begin to see a difference, or, rather, an extension.

With your therapists acting as coaches, you and the other members of the group will begin to role-play parts in situations typical of those you are likely to meet in everyday life. Or even specifically in *your* life, because the group can tailor its role-playing to each member's life needs. You will play-act asking your boss for a raise, saying no to someone who wants you to do a favor, and telling someone to change the way he behaves toward you. You will analyze the way you stand, the tone of your voice, the expression on your face, and any distracting physical gestures—such as tugging at your collar, pulling a strand of your hair, fiddling with your fingers, shuffling your feet, putting your hand over your mouth as you speak. Perhaps you will play back a tape of your performance so that you can hear for yourself whether your voice trailed off at the end of sentences, whether your tone was whiny or pleading, or whether you laughed self-consciously (a real self-putdown!).

At first you will be clumsy. Everyone is. You'll see that confirmed by the role-playing of the other members of the group. But gradually, with your therapists' and the group's encouragement, you will stand taller, speak more clearly, and be able to look the other person in the eye at all times.

Each day you will record in your diary the incidents in which you were—or were not—assertive. And don't expect to be perfect. The important thing is to learn from your mistakes, to analyze them until you know what you did wrong, and then you will do better the next time.

Finding a better way

One of the most difficult things for anyone to do is to tell someone that you don't like the way he is behaving toward you. Take the guy who always wants to have a business lunch —on you.

Now, you could say, "Listen, you, I don't like the way you're ripping me off! Go pick somebody else's pockets." But that wouldn't be assertive. It would be downright abusive, which isn't what you want to achieve.

Instead, your therapist might suggest that you wait until the fellow asks you out to lunch the next time, at which point you might say something like: "You know, when you ask me out to a business lunch and then it ends up on my expense account, I feel pretty resentful toward you."

In that way, you are not condemning the man himself by calling him some sort of a con man. You're simply—and honestly—telling him you don't like his *behavior.*

Now you can use a little muscle. Let him know what you will do if he continues to behave in the same way: "If you do that again, I'll tell the waiter to give the check to you." (And be sure you mean it when you say it.)

Most likely the other person will feel that although you don't like something he has done, you still respect him. Probably he'll say: "All right, this time lunch is on my expense account."

You've won a point, and it feels good, doesn't it? How about pushing for another one, because, really, this matter isn't completely settled yet.

Try negotiating for a compromise: "You know, we really don't discuss much business at these lunches. So why don't we each pay for our own? That way we can just enjoy each other's company."

And chances are he'll agree—because maybe your company is what he wanted in the first place and he just didn't know how to assert himself enough to say so. So enjoy your lunch—and bring your friend to an AT session some time.

Dealing in the truth

One of the most valuable experiences you will have in assertiveness training is being able to express yourself honestly and directly. It's such a relief to let it all out instead of holding it in. Of course, if you said whatever you felt all of the time, you *would* end up hurting someone, because there is a time and a place for that kind of frankness. That is why you also will be trained to discriminate between the times when it would be good for you to assert yourself and the times when it would be too costly. You can be considerate without being a soft touch.

You also can express an opinion without getting into an argument. You can get into a conversation with almost anyone. You can give a word of praise when it is due, and you can accept the praise of others without pretending that you don't deserve it.

This is growth in a very practical, everyday sense. You're avoiding a buildup of resentment—and you're becoming a more sociable person.

Some people complain that AT is mere repetition of words a therapist puts in your mouth, without benefit of any enlightenment about the real cause of your nonassertiveness.

AT therapists, however, point out that repeated success in asserting yourself will make you naturally assertive. And if you don't have the problem any longer, why is it even important to delve into the nature of it?

CHAPTER 14
SILVA MIND CONTROL

It makes you furious, doesn't it?

The interview was going well, and then you were asked to take a typing test and you blew it. You always do. Yet when you aren't under pressure, you're a good typist, fast and accurate. You tried to explain to the interviewer that you were nervous and could do much better if you weren't being tested. But the interviewer smiled that *awful* smile that said, "Sure, sure, they all say that." Naturally, you didn't get the job.

So you stop in a restaurant on the way home and order a big slice of cheesecake. You've been trying to diet for two weeks and you weigh more now than when you began. But what can you do? Something always happens to upset you, and you just *have* to eat. Even when you aren't hungry. In fact, you eat so much, you never give yourself a chance to get hungry.

You were going to stop smoking, too, weren't you? Well, that will have to wait until you're ready for it. Until you're in the mood.

By the time you reach home you have a headache—a bad one. You're irritable, impatient with your family. You lie down and try to relax, but you can't sleep. And if you can't sleep, you'll feel even worse tomorrow. Your headache might even turn into a migraine.

What a rotten day!

Putting you in charge of your mind

Wouldn't you like to be able to take a typing test without going to pieces—and maybe even get the highest score possible?

Wouldn't you like to be able to say no to food you don't need and don't want to eat?

And stop smoking?

And never get those headaches anymore?

And maybe even get a good night's sleep—every night?

Does that sound like an impossible dream? Well, it isn't. You could call it mind over matter—but it's more than that. It's putting you in charge of your mind, and teaching you to make the most of your vast mental powers. That's what Silva Mind Control is all about.

Over 450,000 persons have taken the Silva Mind Control course since it was first offered in 1966. As a growth therapy, it is second only to Transcendental Meditation in popularity. Originally it was developed to help women and men discover and develop mental abilities they never knew they had—and this it still aims to do—but it also has helped people to eliminate compulsive habits such as overeating and smoking; to work more effectively and successfully; to solve specific problems such as finding a lost item, getting out of debt, choosing a more rewarding career, mastering a subject that once was impossibly difficult; to find a friend, a lover, or a mate—and even to find a parking space. It is said to promote leadership qualities, boost self-confidence, and, not surprisingly, overcome shyness.

How?

By teaching you to think on a different level—specifically, your alpha level. And by making you aware that *you are what you think.*

In touch with your own power

Imagine the tangle of telephone wires and cables that crisscross this country. Well, that is simplicity itself compared to the electrical patterns of the human brain. *Your* brain. There are billions of tiny cells in your brain, and each one is hooked up to an intricate electrical communication system. Waves of electrical impulses are constantly sent throughout the brain, giving signals to various brain cells, and the deeper the level of consciousness, the more powerful the signals. Of course, most of the time you aren't aware of all this activity, because you spend most of your time in the upper levels of your consciousness.

But when you are falling asleep, you are reaching down into those deeper levels. In the early portions of your sleep, when you are experiencing a series of active dreams, your brain is functioning at what is called the *alpha* level, which is the source of creative thought. Some amazing things happen there —if only you could recall them. Often you can't.

Now, just think what might happen if you could not only get down to the alpha level while you were awake, but could also direct what happens there. Suppose you could specify the kind of signals to be sent out to other parts of your brain, so that your mind would get to work making your fondest dreams come true?

You can.

Yogis do it. Meditators do it. Biofeedback equipment enables you to do it. And so does Silva Mind Control.

Using Silva Mind Control techniques, you should be able to reach the alpha level of thought while you are awake, even while having a conversation. You should also be able to *program* what goes on there.

Conditioning your consciousness

A Silva Mind Control Course lasts for forty-eight hours and is spread over four successive days (twelve hours each day)— either two weekends or two single weekdays and one weekend. The cost is about two hundred dollars, and you may repeat the course free of charge as many times as you wish. (Many students say that they get even more out of the course the second or third time because their mental powers are so highly developed by the techniques they have learned.)

Bring a blanket with you, because you will spend many of your forty-eight hours lying on the floor, *conditioning* yourself to relax and activate your alpha wave. You will work in a group, with a trainer.

It takes a little time to learn how to shut out the world and reach down into your own mind. But be patient. After you've done it a few times, it will become almost automatic, and you will be able to achieve an alpha state while you are sitting up, walking, talking—almost anywhere, anytime.

The first thing you have to do is lie on the floor in a comfortable position. As you listen to the soothing voice of your trainer describing the mental powers that will soon be yours to command, you begin to descend into your consciousness. Your trainer will count backward from three to one (or from ten to one, depending upon how deeply you want to penetrate your consciousness). And then you are there—in your alpha state.

Now your trainer begins to repeat such phrases as "I can accept or reject anything I am told," "I will use my increasing mental faculties for serving humanity better," and the familiar "Every day in every way, I am getting better and better." This is a reminder that *you* are in control.

Making yourself at home in alpha

As you repeat the conditioning exercises, you will be able to attain your alpha level more quickly. And when you return to your usual level of consciousness, you will feel rested and full of energy. You also will remember everything your trainer told you while you were in alpha.

You're ready for assignments now. The first one is to furnish your alpha *laboratory* in any way you wish. All you need is your imagination. Design an outdoor or indoor scene, anyplace where you will enjoy spending time. Put yourself on a mountaintop or in space, if you like. Create walls or doors or windows anywhere you please. Write notes to yourself on the soft blue sky.

You see—your alpha state can conjure up anything you desire.

Next assignment: *Getting rid of negative thoughts.*

While in your alpha state, think about one of your problems. Picture it.

For example, let's go back to the problem of taking a typing test. Visualize yourself sitting at a typewriter with a timer beside it. See yourself tense, stiff-fingered, defeated. Now imagine that scene surrounded by a blue frame and cancel it out by writing a giant X through it. Then imagine another picture—there you are, all finished with your typing test, holding up a perfect typed page and smiling triumphantly because you have just passed the test. You are relaxed and happy. Put that picture in a white frame and gaze.

You have canceled out that negative image of failure and replaced it with a positive image of success. How you pass the typing test isn't important, and you shouldn't waste time figuring out how you can do it. The point is that you think of yourself as successful—and your thoughts will influence your entire life. You have told your alpha wave to signal your success to other parts of your brain. This means that your mind will start thinking in terms of achieving your goal—and, believe me, your mind will find the way to do it.

That is why, when you think negatively, you program your own failure. But when you think positively, all your energies will move toward whatever you desire.

I know what you're thinking: Wishing makes it so. Well, you know as well as I do that that isn't so. As your Silva trainer will explain to you, wishing for something isn't the same as programming your goal. When you wish, you really don't know whether or not you'll succeed, since you're appealing to a "force" outside your control. There is a certain amount of attendant fear that you may not get what you want. So you create the possibility for failure. Pointing the creative powers of your mind toward what you want is quite different, and more reliable. There is no room for doubt. You aren't hoping you'll get something—you see yourself as already having and enjoying it.

Becoming another

On another assignment your trainer will take you on a fascinating journey. He will ask you to visualize a penny and then to visualize yourself entering it and exploring the inside. You will visualize a wall and pass through it, you will enter a piece of metal. And each time you will experience what it is like to be in such places. You will actually *become* the other.

But that's only the beginning. You will go on to become an animal, perhaps your pet dog or cat, and you will know what that animal is feeling. You will become a friend and know whether he is happy, sad, feeling great, or perhaps not very well.

You will learn to let your mind influence those around you by projecting your good and happy thoughts toward them. Send someone a mental smile—and watch that person smile back at you!

Now do you see why Silva Mind Control insists that you are what you think?

Think healing

The giant X also can be used to get rid of a headache or a cold, to induce sound sleep, and to stop overeating and smoking. And yes, Silva Mind Control students claim they can find parking spaces even in the most impossible places!

One of the most amazing exercises is performed at the end of the forty-eight-hour course. Not every student is able to do it, at least not the first time around, but the results are nevertheless impressive.

You and the other members of the group will pair off. Then you and your partner will go into an alpha state and you will think of a person your partner doesn't even know. You will picture that person clearly and steadily, including as many features as you can possibly remember.

Your partner will concentrate on penetrating your mind and reaching the image you see, just as both of you learned to go through walls or into a penny. This is mind power at its highest.

Your partner may not see anything. Or she may see an image totally different from the one in your mind. But there is a chance—it happens often—that she will be able to describe the very person you are picturing.

She also may be able to detect and diagnose any illness that person has!

Don't be disappointed if you can't do the same. Perhaps you'll make it the next time you take the course.

What you should be able to do, even the first time, is function more effectively, creatively, and energetically.

Silva Mind Control is therefore an excellent way for a person to realize her potential, and this is its greatest appeal. It has been very effective in helping people to break habits such as overeating, smoking, and drinking, but the results are not always permanent. One can, however, simply repeat the training if these habits begin to reappear.

CHAPTER 15 TRANSCENDENTAL MEDITATION

In 1976 a pair of research psychologists conducted a study of two groups of people. The first group of men and women had begun with a very high degree of anxiety, but had been practicing transcendental meditation for six weeks. The second group had begun with only a moderate level of anxiety and had practiced nothing.

The researchers found, somewhat to their amazement, that the first group now had an anxiety level much lower than the second group, which remained pretty much the same. A few weeks later the groups were compared again. And again, the first group's anxiety level had dropped and the second one's hadn't.

The obvious conclusion: Transcendental meditation made the difference.

This is only one test result. There have been many other tests conducted on TM-ers—most with convincing results.

In fact, transcendental meditation—which is *not* a therapy—is now used in conjunction with many forms of psychotherapy and has been found to speed up a patient's ability to recognize and cope with emotional problems. And beyond that, it has proved helpful to what Dr. Harold H. Bloomfield (Director of Psychiatry at the Institute of Psychophysiological Medicine in San Diego, California) calls the " 'average middle-class neurotics' . . . individuals who are not mentally ill, but who, despite material affluence, are unfulfilled.

"Perhaps," says Dr. Bloomfield, "the greatest promise of the TM program is the prospect of helping these millions of dissatisfied people to grow on their own in happiness and achievement without the need for professional assistance."

So far, seven hundred thousand Americans—mainly from among those "middle-class neurotics"—have each paid one hundred and twenty-five dollars to learn the TM technique. And that's not counting the thousands of students who were instructed in TM for nothing, or next to nothing, in TM's early days, when it was considered strictly hippie fare—or the hundreds of thousands who learned how to meditate by reading Dr. Herbert Benson's best-seller, *The Relaxation Response*.

Without a doubt, TM is the most popular, most successful of the growth techniques.

Why?

Because . . .

It is a very simple technique to learn.

Anyone—and everyone—can do it, including children over the age of four.

It is a very pleasant experience.

It produces results almost immediately—and continues to produce more results the longer a person continues practicing it.

The results last—and this is not true of some other growth techniques.

In short, students of TM claim it changes your life—from dissatisfied to satisfied, from unfulfilled to fulfilled, from dull to enthusiastic, from self-defeating to self-actualizing, from withdrawn to outgoing, from frightened to confident, from unhappy to joyous.

Where can you get it?

Everywhere.

Businesses are offering TM courses, free of charge and on company time, to their employees. Many provide meditation rooms.

Schools—even public schools—are beginning to incorporate TM courses in their curricula.

Churches and civic organizations are offering TM courses.

Mental health organizations are sponsoring TM courses.

And, of course, there is the International Meditation Society, founded by the Maharishi Mahesh Yogi, who brought TM to this country in 1959. You can find one of its centers in any major city and in most suburbs.

You can also read Dr. Benson's book, *The Relaxation Response*.

Actually, it would be hard to find a place where TM is not available.

Which is a good thing. Because . . .

TM—the antidote to stress

Even if you haven't read Alvin Toffler's *Future Shock*, you're living it. Your world is changing faster than you can adapt. You are bombarded with more choices than you can consider. You are running into more problems than you can handle—or find the time to solve. You're lucky—and unusual—if you have a place you can call home, if you ever get to know people well enough to call them friends, if you even have a family or can keep in touch with one. You just about learn how to cope with the new when it becomes old, and anything old is not only disposable but must be disposed of. Because if something is not new, then it simply doesn't exist—or so we have come to believe.

So it's Make Way! Make Way! For the New! And Get Rid of the Old! And if you don't keep becoming new, maybe the world will get rid of you too one of these days, right? So you try to keep up, you try to adjust to the new lifestyles and morals and mind sets, even though you're not sure you really want everything that goes with them, even though you may not be comfortable with some of them, and even though you may not really understand what some of them mean. In fact, you may not really know who you are anymore, because you've been trying so hard to become whatever life keeps telling you to be.

No wonder you're anxious. You're living in a world full of stress.

Yes, stress. I know you keep running into that word and you may be tired of it. But that's just the point. You can't avoid it.

"During 40 years of research on stress, I have found no single situation in our lives that is more damaging, more stressful, than that of being faced with a number of alternatives and the necessity of choosing amongst them, but of having no solid criteria upon which to base the decision." So says Dr. Hans Selye, one of the country's leading experts on stress and its effects.

If you're trying to make ends meet, be a good parent, hold your marriage together, keep up with the new information in your field, get ahead in your career, lose weight, make friends, hold on to your temper, get more mileage out of your car, save up for a vacation, meet the right man or woman, cut down on your drinking, get more exercise, get more sleep, fight off a cold, or study for a test, you're under stress.

Maybe you don't have such big problems—a lot of little ones will do the trick, too. Maybe your life is filled with good things —even that can do it.

Stress, defined in TM terms, is "any chemical or physical abnormality in the body . . . caused by overload." It is the primary cause of fatigue today, and by fatigue I mean the kind of exhaustion that even twelve to fourteen hours of sleep won't cure. You know the feeling. You go to bed early, fall asleep right away, and then wake up feeling more tired than ever. That's because your sleep didn't go deep enough, and your stress kept on churning all night.

According to the Maharishi Mahesh Yogi, "Rest is the basis of all activity." In other words, how well we perform is directly related to how rested we feel. And the more fatigued we become under the pressure of stress, the less able we are to deal with that stress. Nasty, isn't it?

What you need is a deeper kind of rest than ordinary sleep provides. You also need a new source of energy.

Transcendental meditation offers you both.

Achieving restful alertness

If you are interested in transcendental meditation, you can attend two introductory lectures free of charge and without any obligation to commit yourself to the training. They are available almost daily and nightly in every TM center across the country and, indeed, the world. An instructor will explain to you that during meditation your body will require far less oxygen, and that your metabolic rate will decrease much more, and much faster, than when you are asleep. Your mind, however, will remain fully alert—a condition known in TM as *restful alertness.* (This claim has been confirmed by medical experimenters who have studied persons using TM.)

Your instructor will also tell you that deep within the mind there is a source of pure energy from which all thoughts originate. It is called the *source of thought.* Ordinarily, in your everyday way of thinking, you bypass this energy source because you spend most of your thinking time on a more superficial level of consciousness, and most of the thoughts originating at the deeper level never get as far as the surface because they are crowded out by all the distractions of your life. But if you can learn to reach down and tap this source of energy and thought, your whole manner of thinking and living will change. And this is what TM will enable you to do.

You can learn the technique of transcendental meditation in four sessions—one of them individual and the other three in a group. During the individual session, your instructor will give you your personal mantra (a Sanskrit sound you think to yourself to focus your thoughts during meditation), which is not to be revealed to anyone, ever. He will also teach you how to meditate. Believe me, it's easy. Amazingly easy.

Sitting in a comfortable position, with eyes closed, you will focus on your mantra. Other thoughts will come into your mind, but you won't fight them. You'll just allow them to pass through your mind and go on their way. You may even veer away from your mantra now and then, but that's all right. Get back to it and continue where you left off.

Gradually your mantra will become larger. It will fill every corner of your awareness until finally the two of you become one. You have reached the TM state of *no-mind,* where all is quiet, where you have no thoughts, no feelings, no troubles, no awareness of your body. You have completely quieted your mind. More than that, you have *transcended* it. You are in touch with your source of thought, and there is no end to the energy you find there.

In about twenty minutes you'll feel the meditation ending by itself. Slowly you become aware of your mantra again. You sense your body, your physical surroundings. And you feel absolutely relaxed and rested.

During your three group sessions, which each last about two hours, you will practice meditating under the guidance of an instructor. After that you will have the tools to work on your own, although you may go back for rechecking at any time.

It is essential that you meditate for twenty minutes twice a day, once in the morning and once in the afternoon or evening. You should not meditate just before bedtime, because you will find the experience so refreshing and invigorating that you won't be able to sleep. Nor should you meditate less than two hours after eating, since while you're slowing down your metabolic rate you slow down your digestion.

When you have learned the technique and go on to meditate on your own, choose a room where you will be free from distractions. Leave the lights on or turn them off, whichever makes you more comfortable.

And that's all there is to it.

Except that . . .

You may feel a bit restless the first time you meditate. That's okay. It won't last. When you have meditated a few times you will begin to notice a difference. Your twenty minutes will pass very quickly. You will have fewer and fewer interrupting thoughts. You will experience a deeper sense of peace and contentment.

After four or five sessions you will feel as if you have made contact with yourself—not the self that tries to adapt to the world's demands, but the pure core of your basic being. It's like meeting an old friend, and yet there is a newness about it. You will feel yourself flowing along with your own rhythms, your own directions. *This is the center of your life.* This is the part of you that knows who you really are. What a welcome change it is to let it point the way for you (inner-directed), rather than being pushed and pulled every which way by external diversions (outer-directed), such as your job, TV, the kids, decisions, problems, change, and you name it.

Ritual, not religion

When you receive your mantra, you participate in an initiation ceremony. Barefoot and kneeling before a picture of Guru Dev, the teacher of the Maharishi Mahesh Yogi, you must place an offering of fruit and flowers upon an altar while your instructor chants in Sanskrit.

This ceremony bothers some people, who feel that it places TM in the category of religion. It so bothered the Nationwide Coalition for Religious Integrity that it filed suit to stop TM classes offered in five New Jersey public schools. The suit was based on the charge that TM has been "camouflaged as a secular science" in order to qualify for taxpayer funds and attract a wider following.

Representatives of the TM organization deny that TM is a religion. "It does not require faith and it does not require worship," they say.

Some impressive claims

For several years, the only tests of TM's effectiveness in combating the stress of contemporary life were conducted by the International Meditation Society or were published by the Maharishi International University Press—and consequently were eyed with skepticism. But during the past few years scientists who conducted independent tests have confirmed the original findings. And they are impressive. For example:

When persons suffering from high blood pressure used TM, for anywhere from four to sixty-three weeks, their blood pressure levels dropped markedly.

After thirty days of TM, persons who had been insomniacs were able to fall asleep within fifteen minutes.

TM practitioners have lower levels of anxiety and higher degrees of inner control.

Over a twenty-one-month period, alcohol and cigarette users (both heavy and light users) were able to cut down substantially on drinking and smoking.

TM has helped drug users to cut down and sometimes eliminate their dependence upon legal and illegal drugs.

Psychotherapists have found TM a significant aid in the treatment of depression and obsessive-compulsive behavior.

And many students say it has enabled them to function more successfully, meaningfully, lovingly, and happily.

CHAPTER 16
BODY TECHNIQUES: THE BODY/MIND CONNECTION

Have you ever noticed that when you're on vacation, perhaps lying on the beach of a tropical island, enjoying the delicious sun, your troubles just seem to vanish? Your office seems far away, your piled-up desk doesn't matter, and all the pressure of your life back home seems too unreal to worry about. You can't even think about such things for more than a few seconds. You'd much rather stretch and turn onto your other side. Or go for a swim. Or play tennis. Or jog. Or do nothing at all except go on relaxing.

But then your vacation ends and you have to go back to the pressure. You aren't home for more than a few hours and you're tense, anxious, worried, restless, sleepless—and *tired.* Now it's the beach and the warm sun that seem far away. Relaxation? Ridiculous! Who can relax?

Yet you can't help thinking, *Wouldn't it be wonderful if I could feel as peaceful, rested, and strong as I did lying there on the sand?*

You can.

You don't have to wait until your next vacation, either.

You can feel refreshed and relaxed right in the middle of your high-pressured, everyday life, by using techniques that emphasize working on your body to help you feel better from the inside out.

A logical approach

There is a connection between the health and well-being of the body and that of the mind. When you're physically tired, your mind doesn't function as well. When you're under mental stress, your body may ache all over. So it is important, when one part of ourselves isn't performing as well as it should, that we treat not only the obvious symptoms but the rest of ourselves as well. This is called a *holistic* approach to good health, and it is the basis for body/mind techniques. They promote the well-being of the whole person through the improvement of the body as well as the mind.

When your body is completely relaxed—such as when you are on the beach—you cannot also be tense. The two are mutually exclusive. So if your body is relaxed, say the body technique practitioners, your mind will feel relaxed as well.

Therefore, the first aim of a body technique is to teach you how to relax your body—thereby preventing the stresses in your life from getting hold of your mind, from twisting you into a tense, rigid pretzel.

The second aim of a body technique is to undo the harm your emotional and mental anxieties have done to your body. Frustration, fear, tension, anger, depression, and all the other negative feelings you have experienced over the years have caused you to slouch, distribute your weight unevenly, stick out your chest, tilt forward or backward, and make an uncertain contact with the ground beneath your feet. And when your body isn't properly aligned, it doesn't function as well as it was meant to. Even if you were to clear up your psychological problems, your body still would bear the marks of previous strain—and if your body can't relax, the rest of you can't either.

A third aim of a body technique—or, rather, of *some* body techniques—is to uncover the cause of psychological illness by treating the distortions they have caused in the body.

A fourth aim of a body technique is to make you aware of your body and of the way it moves when its parts are properly aligned. Once you know how this feels, you will be able to keep your body relaxed and healthy, thereby preventing stress and anxiety from gaining a foothold in your life.

A fifth aim is to teach you how to tap your physical reserves of energy so that you can do more and do it more effectively.

A mixed bag

Some body techniques are almost exclusively physical exercises. Some combine exercise with forms of meditation and visualization. Some include massage, dance, and special diets.

Some you can do yourself, and some must be done to you. And some hurt—although in most instances the techniques emphasize fluid movement rather than strenuous exertion.

All body techniques, however, have one thing in common: a physical route to psychological health.

CHAPTER 17
BIOENERGETICS

Is your body trying to tell you something?

Quite possibly it is, and if so, you'd better pay attention.

Stand in front of a mirror and take a look at your shoulders. No, they certainly aren't slouching. In fact, they're held back very rigid. Why is that? Are you angry about something?

You aren't? You don't have a gripe in the world? Are you sure? (You look pretty angry right now. And you're shouting at me, insisting that you're not the least bit angry.)

Ooh, look at your shoulders in the mirror. They're up so high and your head is down, almost as if you were cowering in fear.

You aren't aware of that, are you? And yet you feel a vague sense of anxiety.

And you—notice the soft expression in your eyes. You seem very friendly until I look at your jaw, which is stuck out a mile. That tells me you're defiant, which doesn't match the expression in your eyes. You've got a conflict, my friend.

I could go on and on, but I think the point has already been made: Your body describes your feelings—to anyone who knows how to read it.

The examples I've just mentioned are simple, fairly obvious physical indications of psychological states. Most of us are accustomed to looking at a person's face for clues to her emotions. We notice whether she fiddles with her fingers, crosses and uncrosses her legs, tugs at herself or buttons, hunches over or sits straight up. But there are other more subtle, complicated forms of body expressions which only the trained mind can interpret. For instance, the way a person breathes—shallowly or from deep down in her abdomen—reveals a lot about her emotional health.

So say the bioenergetic therapists.

Sex and energy

Bioenergetics began with Wilhelm Reich (1897–1957), who was a promising student of Sigmund Freud's until the two of them parted company over a difference of opinion. Freud believed that sexual drives should be controlled by the ego, for the good of society. Reich, convinced that the sex instinct was the source of all biological energy, passionately advocated the fulfillment of sexual desires. He openly urged sexual relations for troubled adolescents and extramarital affairs for discordant marriages.

After breaking with Freud, Reich formulated his own kind of therapy, which was half psychoanalytical and half physical. He and his patient would discuss the patient's early childhood during part of their sessions, and spend the rest of the time looking for physical clues to emotional blocks.

Reich believed that if the sexual desires were blocked, or repressed, by the ego (which represents our rationality), then the body would be deprived of vital life energy. When sexuality was repressed, other feelings were repressed along with it. The pain, frustration, depression, rage, and fear caused by repression would ultimately show up as areas of weakness or tension in the body. Usually the patient was not specifically aware of these disorders, nor was he aware of his body's lifelessness until the therapist pointed them out. As the therapist massaged the afflicted areas or instructed the patient to assume certain postures that brought pressure on the areas, the patient often remembered traumatic experiences going far back into his early childhood. If, under the therapist's guidance, the patient was able to bring his related emotions into the open, he experienced both psychological and physical relief.

As bizarre as Reich's methods were considered in his day, they have become the foundation for many of the psychophysical forms of therapy we know now.

For example, Reich was a very active therapist who would provoke a patient to anger in order to help him release his pent-up rage. He would massage the patient's body so vigorously at times that he caused pain, which he claimed was emotional pain inflicted long ago and imprisoned in the patient's body. Bioenergetic analysts still alternate between discussions with the patient and direct physical contact. Reich's patients were partly or completely unclothed, so that their physical tensions were always apparent. This is not always so today.

Updating the technique

Wilhelm Reich was too much of a maverick to form a school or organize a following who would carry on his work after him. His research might have died with him had it not been for Dr. Alexander Lowen, who took up Reich's study of a sound mind in a sound body, coined the term *bioenergetics*, and smoothed out some of the wrinkles in Reich's techniques. Under Lowen's leadership, bioenergetics became a respectable, effective therapy.

Originally Lowen worked with schizophrenics, who have an acute lack of awareness of their bodies. (They are not always aware that their feet are on the floor, and may stumble a great deal, especially on stairs. Their sense of direction is poor, and they often seem to have lost their way.) When the bioenergetic techniques were successful, Lowen began to apply them to patients with various forms of neurosis. Eventually he realized that even well-adjusted people would benefit from an increased ability to express their emotions freely and physically.

So if you're the type who has too rigid a hold on your feelings, if you have difficulty getting close to others and the possibility of intimacy scares you, and even if you suffer from inner fears and anxieties for reasons you don't understand, bioenergetics may be able to help. This form of therapy is also especially effective in treating sex problems.

The method

The first thing you have to do in bioenergetic therapy is find out what your ego has been repressing, and then you have to get your ego to let go.

You begin with certain diagnostic exercises, or *postures*, designed to reveal to you and your therapist where your weak spots are. At first they may seem difficult, even uncomfortable. In one of them you will be told to stand with your feet about thirty inches apart, your toes turned slightly inward, and your clenched fists pressed against the small of your back. Then you will be told to arch your body backward as far as possible. For a bioenergetically integrated person, this should be a fairly comfortable position, but if you suffer from a neurosis, some odd things may happen. Your pelvis may twist to one side; you may fall over; you may not be able to arch your back. This is your body telling you where the pain is. For instance, pressure in the pelvic area may indicate sexual problems or fears.

But if you don't have any severe repression, you will begin to sense your body's aliveness—and you will be somewhat surprised that you never sensed it before. Your thigh muscles will begin to pulsate after a while, which is a very pleasant experience. It tells you that your body has a life of its own—and maybe you should allow yourself to enjoy its sensations.

Now you go on to more-active exercises.

Your therapist will tell you to strike a hard rubber bed as hard as you can—you can even use a tennis racket, if you wish. You should also shout whatever angry words or thoughts come into your mind.

But you resist. You feel a little foolish slamming a bed for no reason at all. Indeed, maybe you can't express your anger. You might feel more than foolish—you might feel incapable of this kind of acting-out. So you say you're not angry at anything.

Nonsense, says your therapist. Everybody is angry at something.

Well, you try. You slap the bed a few times—and then you really get into it. Something has come over you and you're mad! Mad as hell! You don't know why, but it feels so good to let it out, to strike that mattress as hard as you possibly can. Now here's what is happening: Your physical actions are stimulating your repressed anger to such a degree that your ego is giving in to the pressure and letting go. Your body work is releasing the blocks in your mind.

You begin to curse and shout, and before you know it you are telling your therapist about an incident that happened long ago. You didn't even know you remembered it. But here it is, right in front of you. Maybe you hate your parents or a brother or a sister for the way they treated you when you were a child. The image is vivid now. Maybe you blame a parent for dying and leaving you abandoned. Maybe you're angry because you didn't get enough love. You can picture images of the past, images released by the simple action of unleashing your anger. Whatever it is, you can deal with it now. You have the perspective of adulthood. You're not a small child at the mercy of giants who can manipulate you in whichever ways they please.

Finally, it's time for discussion, for analysis of the feelings you have just unblocked. Releasing them is only the first step; recognizing them as part of yourself is the necessary conclusion. You don't want your anger to be repressed again, so you allow your therapist to help you accept your real feelings, no matter how disagreeable they may be.

For serious problems and neuroses, count on at least a year of therapy. If you just want to feel better about yourself and be more in tune with your body, therapy will be shorter. Either way, you will meet with your therapist for one hour a week at a cost of anywhere from twenty-five to seventy dollars per session. You'll spend time releasing the feelings and then dealing with them through discussion.

As is the case with any therapy or school of treatment, there are some skeptics. Some psychotherapists feel that bioenergetics places too much emphasis on the release of emotions and not enough on understanding the reasons for their original repression. Some also point out that too often parents are blamed for neuroses that may have been caused by other factors in the patient's environment. For instance, the trauma may have been caused not by what actually happened but by what the patient *imagined* happened. A few critics complain that the close physical relationship of patient and therapist leaves the patient especially vulnerable to manipulation and quackery, and caution prospective patients to look into the therapists' credentials carefully.

CHAPTER 18
BIOFEEDBACK TRAINING

Maybe you saw it happen.

Maybe you were watching the Montreal Olympics on TV during the summer of 1976, when a young Japanese gymnast fell and broke his knee. You could just imagine the pain he must have felt.

If you saw that, you must have been amazed—as were thousands of viewers—when that same young man came back the next day and won a medal for his performance on the rings.

How did he do it? Olympics rules forbid any kind of anesthesia or drugs. The pain in his knee must have been agonizing—was he able to ignore it? Are such things possible?

It *is* amazing, and it *is* possible, although, I must admit, the young gymnast's example was an extraordinary example of mind over matter. But you and I and everybody have done similar things, without realizing it.

Mind over body

Did you ever pick up something that was much too heavy for you to carry, even for a short distance? You felt your grip giving way, but then you *willed* some strength into your arms and hands and managed to get as far as you had to go.

Did you ever run for a bus just as it was pulling away from the curb? You're not much of a runner and you had already run for a whole block. You were huffing and puffing, and your lungs were about to burst—but you managed to speed up somehow and catch your bus.

Did you ever remain alert and attentive during a three-day

sales conference? When it was all over, you collapsed with fatigue and you wondered how you ever got through it, but somehow you did.

Did you ever come down with a sore throat on the day you had a speaking engagement? You felt that nasty scratchiness coming on, but you made up your mind that your voice would hold out until you finished speaking. And it did!

How did you do those things?

You don't know?

Well, neither does anyone else.

Scientists know only that it *does* happen, that there is a liaison between mind and body which makes it possible for one to influence the other in amazing ways.

An accidental discovery

During the 1960s Dr. Barbara Brown was conducting a study in a California Veterans Administration Hospital when she stumbled onto a phenomenon that she later described as *biofeedback*. Dr. Brown was demonstrating the activity of brain waves to a group of patients. She was using an electroencephalograph (EEG) and had attached a light to it so that each time the patient generated an alpha wave the light would go on. The patient could see the light and was therefore aware whether he was in a beta state of normal thought or the restful, dreamlike alpha state.

Originally Dr. Brown simply wanted to record the reactions of persons to different colors. But then she noticed that as her subjects began to identify the pleasant sensations of the alpha state with the EEG signals, they actually were able to produce more alpha waves—*at will!*

The brain waves are like heartbeat, respiration, and many other functions of the body in that they are considered autonomic, or involuntary—meaning that we don't have any conscious control over them. When we're cold, our body temperature goes down, and when we're hot, it goes up—and there isn't anything we can do about it.

Or so we used to think.

But maybe we *can* do something. At least, that's what Dr. Brown thought. So she continued her study. She found that the more a patient knew about the way his body functioned, the more he could control it. For instance, after a few hours with the EEG a patient could increase his beta waves to achieve greater levels of alertness, or his alpha waves to induce relaxation.

Awareness equals control

In recent years there have been many other fascinating experiments indicating that the mind can regulate even the involuntary functions of the body. A person suffering from a severe headache, even a migraine, can learn to direct the flow of blood away from her throbbing head and relieve the pressure causing the pain. Mountain climbers in cold temperatures have been able to increase the temperature of their hands to prevent them from freezing.

How?

We don't know, any more than we know how the young gymnast performed in spite of a broken knee. Or how you and I have done some of the things we do when we "put our mind to it."

We do know that when we become aware of how we function—specifically, when we realize how our bodies feel as we function—we can, in a sense, will that feeling to occur again, and with it the bodily function that produces that feeling. And the process of becoming aware and then producing the function is called *biofeedback training*.

In short, it means that with the aid of certain machinery our bodies are capable of telling us how they are functioning at a certain time, and that our minds are capable of telling our bodies what we *want* them to do.

Gaining control of your body

If you are interested in biofeedback training, you should know that you will need at least eight to fourteen hour-long sessions with a private BFT practitioner to learn how to control a bodily function in order to feel better. The cost is about thirty-five dollars per hour, although some biofeedback centers affiliated with medical schools may agree to treat you without cost if your problem fits into one of their current studies. Either way, if you are also under the care of a doctor you must have that doctor's approval of the BFT training before you will be accepted.

The machines used are fairly simple devices connected to a bell or light or some other indicator you can hear or observe. You are seated in a comfortable chair or lie on a bed. Attached to various parts of your body are sensitive contacts from the biofeedback machine, held in place by tape.

You are probably wondering how it feels to be hooked up into machines such as an EEG, which records changes in brain waves, or an electromyograph, which records changes in muscle tension. Well, it doesn't hurt.

The first thing you have to do is relax. But suppose you can't? Suppose that's your problem? You're always tense, anxious, and that's why you're here.

Okay.

You can't relax. And because you can't, that buzzer attached to the machine is making an irritating noise. You wish your therapist would turn it off. But she won't. She wants you to do it. However, she may suggest various ways in which you can help yourself to relax, such as visualizing your muscles loosening up.

At first you may become more tense than ever, especially with that buzzer going all the time. But every now and then, as you concentrate on your muscles—perhaps on only one at a time—the buzzer will stop, indicating that you are achieving muscular relaxation. That may last only for a moment, but it does give you an awareness of two things: the sensation associated with muscular relaxation and your mind's ability to control your body.

Gradually, as you complete more sessions with your therapist, you will be able to turn off that buzzer for more than a moment. Finally you will make it keep still for as long as you please.

But then what?

You can't very well go through life attached to that machine, can you? Of course not.

Your training isn't complete until you can accomplish muscular relaxation at will *without the aid of a machine*. And that is how you will spend the rest of your hours with your therapist—you will practice exerting the same mind power over your body, but without the machine. You don't need the buzzer anymore, because you already know how it *feels* when you no longer have muscle tension. And when you will that feeling, your body makes it happen and your mind relaxes.

When BFT helps

BFT requires a lot of patience, and it is expensive, but it has been proved helpful in treating many physical and psychological ailments, such as headache, backache, asthma, insomnia, menstrual pains, muscular tension, epilepsy, fatigue, drug and alcohol addiction, sexual dysfunction, anxiety, high blood pressure, stroke, paralysis, and chronic pain. One of its most remarkable achievements is in the rehabilitation of muscles paralyzed by stroke.

Beware the imitation BFT

BFT is a serious scientific study still in its infancy, but already it has attracted so much attention that it is considered by many people to be a fad. And, like anything else that looks like a fad, it has its quick-buck merchandisers.

No doubt you have seen ads for mood rings and other pieces of jewelry that are supposed to change color according to the body temperature (and mood) of the wearer. Well, no harm done. But the same can't be said about some "brain-wave machines" put on the market and advertised as a do-it-yourself form of BFT. Some machines do no more than measure movements of the scalp and eyebrows, but one machine led its buyers to produce an epileptic brain-wave pattern.

So watch out. BFT is *not* a do-it-yourself project. It must be attempted only with the aid of professionals. It isn't the simplest or cheapest of the body methods, but, in the opinion of many scientists associated with its pioneering work, it may be the great healing discovery of the future.

CHAPTER 19
ROLFING

Ida Rolf, the eighty-six-year-old originator of the deep-massage technique known as Rolfing, says that its success rate is "100 percent if it is done properly."

Not everyone agrees.

"It's a crock," says one man who has been Rolfed.

An osteopath calls it an "unscientific application of massage. You can't do much harm with it, but I can't see it on a scientific basis."

On the other hand, a public relations executive says that Rolfing cured the pain in her foot after several other kinds of therapy failed to help.

A young mother says that although Rolfing gave her more energy, poise, and self-confidence, she has doubts about allowing her eight-year-old son to be Rolfed.

"It's too painful—I couldn't stand it," says a young man who went through four sessions and then quit.

"It hurt—but what a relief it brought!" says another, who completed all the sessions.

Despite these differences of opinion, over thirty thousand persons have paid forty to fifty dollars per session for a series of ten sessions lasting sixty to seventy-five minutes each. They have allowed themselves to be stretched, elbowed, pummeled, and massaged until some of them cried—and most of them are grateful for the experience.

Why?

Because, they claim, they feel much better, not only physically but emotionally.

In the steps of Wilhelm Reich

Ida Rolf believes, as did Wilhelm Reich, that psychological traumas afflict the body as well as the psyche. We start out our lives with a well-integrated body, designed and balanced to work with the law of gravity. If we develop in a healthy, problem-free way, we stand straight but relaxed, with most of our weight close to an imaginary vertical line that could be drawn from head to feet. However, usually that doesn't last long. As we react to the stresses and frustrations of life, we develop a characteristic posture that reveals how we deal with those life situations. Some of us are hunched forward (defeated), some seem to be flinching away from an expected blow (afraid), some stick out our chin (aggressive), and some puff up our chest (threatening). Feet get turned inward, knees buckle, pelvises tip forward or backward, one shoulder is thrust out farther than the other, to name only a few common posture distortions.

Gravity—friend or foe?

There are purely physical causes that shift our bodies away from that vertical line.

Who didn't fall off a bicycle or a horse or a fence at least once as a child? If you just got a bruise, that wasn't so bad. But maybe you twisted an ankle and had to shift most of your weight to one foot for a few days, or even a few weeks. When your ankle healed, you were back to normal, or so you thought. Actually, you weren't.

When you hurt your ankle and had to take some weight off it, the tissue connecting the ankle muscles (fascia) began to thicken and shorten from disuse. And when you were able to put your weight back on that foot, the fascia never recovered. It remained short and thick. You didn't walk with a limp, but you were off center nevertheless, and your body was now working against, rather than with, gravity.

Gravity is a lot stronger than you are, so it took a lot of your energy to fight it, even though you were losing the battle. That meant you had to do with less energy somewhere else, possibly in your emotional life, and when problems arose you weren't able to deal with them successfully. Probably you weren't conscious of your emotional handicaps, but they in turn affected the way your body developed in response to the way you felt. If you were afraid, or angry, or depressed, your body began to reflect it. That wonderful alignment of all your parts began to disintegrate, giving gravity more of an edge in its attempt to pull you down. And on and on it went . . .

Until you developed an ache here, or a pain there, or you got tired easily or felt clumsy, or just didn't like the way you stood, walked, or sat. All of which are the reasons most people turn to Rolfing.

Perhaps you went to more than one doctor and tried several kinds of treatment, with no alleviation of your discomfort. Perhaps some therapists agreed with you that there was something wrong, but couldn't correct it, and perhaps someone told you that your aches and pains were imaginary.

So you decided to try Rolfing, almost as a last resort. But that's the way most people approach Rolfing, because, after all, it does seem pretty kinky. At least from a distance.

Ouch!

Yes, Rolfing does hurt. Sometimes a lot.

But the hurt doesn't last long after the session is over.

The reason Rolfing hurts is that the Rolfer massages your body on a very deep level. He reaches down into the core of those distorted fascias and actually stretches them back into shape and function. And if he is a qualified, thoroughly trained Rolfer, he has an extraordinary knowledge of anatomy and musculature, so he knows how to massage without causing physical damage.

For the first six or eight sessions the Rolfer will dig into specific trouble spots, working on the fascias connecting the muscles that are not properly in place. Then, during the final sessions, he will realign all the parts of your body until you will be able to stand, sit, and walk as well as a young child. Your weight will once again be close to an imaginary vertical line drawn from the top of your head down through your body to your feet, which will rest firmly on the ground. You will feel taller, lighter, and much more flexible.

You also will have much more energy, because you will not be wasting your strength fighting gravity.

So much for the physical aspects of Rolfing. There also are psychological benefits.

Sometimes, when a Rolfer is working with fascias that are extremely thick and short, the patient encounters a lot of pain, which in turn seems to release pent-up emotions the patient has long forgotten. As the Rolfer continues massaging, he and the patient discuss these feelings. Long-buried traumas are relived and put into perspective, old fears and longings are dissipated, the causes of compulsions are uncovered and understood—and once these things are brought into the open, they no longer are able to handicap the person. They are replaced by a feeling of emotional freedom that corresponds to the sense of physical freedom experienced in a well-integrated body. (Rolfers call it *structural integration.*)

For those who do not have unconscious difficulties to bring to light, Rolfing still seems to have a psychological bonus. Perhaps it is only natural that when we can move freely and comfortably we feel more poised and self-confident. Anyway, this seems to be the common experience of those who have been Rolfed. "It was worth the pain," they say.

CHAPTER 20
YOGA

A friend of mine is taking an adult education course in yoga exercises at her local high school. She wants to shape up after a winter of too much food and too little physical activity.

A colleague, a doctor with a fast-growing practice, is studying yogic breathing with a small group under the guidance of a guru. He wants to get rid of tension.

A few of my friends and I get together at my house every Tuesday evening to practice yoga and meditate, with a little visualization thrown in. We want to reach deeper levels of consciousness.

A young man I know got so interested in yoga that he gave up his job and went to live in an ashram, a community of men and women who practice the more complicated precepts of yoga on a twenty-four-hour-a-day basis. He wants a more spiritual level of existence.

Yoga means different things to different people, which is one reason why it is hard to describe. Some people call it a religion; some deny that it is and say it is a method. Some see it as a type of exercise to make the body more flexible, and some think of it as a way of breathing. Some think of it as a form of self-denial and self-sacrifice bordering on the masochistic, and some consider it a kick young people have to get out of their systems.

And then there are those who think of yoga as a way to walk barefoot over hot coals, or charm a serpent by playing a flute, or even vanish in a puff of smoke—images no doubt influenced by watching old movies in the wee hours of the morning.

However you look at it, yoga is a fascinating group of disciplines. It can be traced back in time to around 3000 B.C., making it the oldest self-help program by far. Yet it fits neatly into contemporary life—and offers something for just about anyone.

"Peace"

According to an ancient legend, a powerful king once asked a wise old yogi, "What is happiness?" And the yogi smiled and answered, "Peace."

Today we're still asking that same question, with a desperate urgency. And the answer is the same.

You know the saying—"There's nothing new under the sun"? Well, here's another example of its truth. We think of stress as a strictly current phenomenon, as a product of our times, right? Yet thousands of years ago yoga philosophers recognized tension as one of the major problems of human existence. Some of them described it as a vampire living within the body and feeding off its life force. To deal with tension and counteract the ravages of stress, they concluded, a person needed to achieve a state of inner peace and serenity that could not be shattered by internal conflicts or external problems. So they devised a system of exercises to help people develop inner peace.

Becoming a together person

Beginning with the exercises that promote physical flexibility, the student of yoga can go on to attain mental and spiritual well-being, all three of which are the essence of yoga. For the word itself—*yoga*—is a derivation of an ancient Sanskrit word meaning *union:* body, mind, and spirit working together to develop their highest potential, and then reaching into the cosmos to unite the person with what is variously described as the Godhead, the Essence of Existence, the Cosmic Consciousness, the Infinite, Truth, and the Ultimate Reality. To some this means a deity (which is why yoga is often considered to be a religion); to some it is nature, morality, perfection, among others.

Quite a goal! And not one to be tackled alone—which is where the word *guru* comes in.

A guru is a teacher of yoga, and not all of them are celebrities. Most gurus are humble, dedicated practitioners of yoga whose lives are supposed to be lessons in themselves. In fact, one of the most demanding yoga precepts is that of working "without seeking the fruits of that work," or, in other words, serving without thought of recompense.

You don't have to see a guru privately, à la some rock stars. Yoga can be taught very well in a group, at very modest fees. You also can learn yoga at some health spas for slightly higher fees, but still not expensive. It is one of the most reasonable self-development courses you can find—and you can find it everywhere these days. The important thing is to find an authentic yoga program and not a watered-down version, because yoga, to be effective, must be done properly.

The right way for you

One of the most confusing aspects of yoga is that there are various, different ways of practicing it, all of them leading to the same goal of union with the higher forces of life. The reason for these differences is that not all of us are the same, nor are we all capable of following the same path to that goal. So, in the wisdom of the great old masters, there are different roads for different kinds of people. Take your choice:

Hatha yoga is the form most Westerners use and is concerned with attaining physical health through proper breathing, bodily postures, and concentration.

Karma yoga is the practice of selfless service and the achievement of such unity with the divine consciousness that the person becomes the instrument for the desires of that consciousness.

Bhakti yoga is the constant devotion to God or to a teacher—to the point where the individual loses awareness of her own being.

Raja yoga is a way of gaining control of the mind through meditation and concentration exercises.

Japa yoga is similar to raja yoga in emphasizing meditation, but includes the repetition of a mantra (Sanskrit sound) to make the practitioner more mindful of the higher force.

Jnana yoga is the development of an awareness of the divine force within the self.

Laya yoga is mastery of the mind and will.

Kriya yoga is the attainment of daily body control, mental development, and thoughts pleasing to God.

Tantra yoga is a ritualized form of sex through which two people lose their sense of ego and become one—with each other and with the cosmos.

Kundalini yoga is the development of psychic power through special breathing techniques and a combination of raja yoga meditation and hatha yoga physical development.

You may study any or all of these so-called pathways. Any one, properly done, is said to lead the student to the ultimate yoga goal—union of the material self with the powerful spiritual forces of the universe.

Many people find that a little yoga leads to a lot more. It isn't unusual for a person to start out studying exercises and become so interested in other areas of yoga that he goes on to study meditation and breathing. Some go on to special diets and observe the finer points of yogic philosophy. All of which is fine, if it helps you. But heed a word of caution from Indra Devi (in *Yoga for Americans*), who did much to make yoga popular in the United States:

"The advanced stages of yoga require many years of special

preparation—practices for which the American mode of living, its tempo and surroundings, are not well suited. Under existing circumstances these advanced practices may prove dangerous and detrimental to your physical and mental wellbeing and balance. It is better, therefore, to leave them alone and to limit yourself to the practice of the yoga postures and deep breathing and relaxation exercises, with some of the time devoted to concentration and meditation."

It's all in the breathing

Those seemingly impossible yoga exercises are based upon flexibility, not exertion, and they take a long time to master. The most important part of all yoga postures is proper breathing, and this is the first thing you will learn as a yoga student.

Normally we think of breathing as inhale, exhale, but your yoga instructor will tell you that there are actually four stages to proper breathing: inhale, hold, exhale, hold. When you inhale, your blood pressure goes up slightly and the arteries leading to your heart narrow. When you exhale, your blood pressure goes down a bit and your arteries expand. By holding the inhale and the exhale, you allow more time for each of these physiological processes to occur more thoroughly, which makes it possible for oxygen to permeate the bloodstream and for impurities to be removed. Yoga practitioners also claim that by slowing down our breathing, we reduce tension almost immediately.

There are many kinds of meditating techniques practiced in yoga. Some combine meditation with visualization and special yogic postures.

Total health

According to enthusiasts, there is hardly anything that can't be cured or improved through the practice of yoga. A combination of exercises, proper breathing, and meditation is said to bring relief from stress, high blood pressure, ulcers, insomnia, drug addiction, respiratory difficulties, and heart conditions. It also is said to control jealousy, anger, grief, hatred, frustration, shyness, nervousness, and stage fright. One of the more interesting claims is that it slows the aging process.

CHAPTER 21
est

As the author of *est: 60 Hours That Transform Your Life*, I have to admit to a preference. Personally, I think est is marvelous, and you should be aware of that right now.

est, which stands for Erhard Seminars Training—also the Latin verb meaning *it is*—doesn't fit into any of the other categories we have discussed. It is not a therapy, nor does it attempt to solve problems. Neither does it aim to change a person.

As est founder Werner Erhard put it, "Sometimes people get the notion that the purpose of est is to make you better. It is not. I happen to think that you are perfect exactly the way you are . . . The problem is that people get stuck acting the way they *were*, instead of being the way they are."

And so est offers the trainee a *transformation* rather than an improvement or a cure. According to est president Don Cox, the training transforms:

1. One's experience of experiencing.
2. One's experience of knowing.
3. One's experience of self.

Doubletalk as method

Seems confusing, doesn't it?

But somehow you got the message, right?

Actually, you *experienced* the message—which is what est is all about.

"Each person experiences the training in his own way," an est pamphlet explains. "After you take the training, you probably won't know *how* it works; you will only know *that* it works."

Life, the est instructors will tell you, cannot be put into words. One has to experience it directly. And one of the reasons why people are so dissatisfied today is that they have accepted other people's verbal versions of reality instead of finding out what it is all about for themselves.

Some other est aphorisms are:

"The truth doesn't mean anything. It just is."

"If you keep saying it the way it really is, eventually your word is law in the universe."

"I know that you know that I love you. What I want you to know is that I know you love me."

(Werner Erhard talking.)

Seems like doubletalk, doesn't it? Yet its convoluted logic is deliberate, and after you have taken the course it all begins to make sense.

The main focus of est, you see, is to have you experience that you, and you alone, are responsible for your life. Whatever has happened to you from the moment of your birth is your own doing. You planned it. You make it happen. Or, as an est instructor will tell you, happy or miserable as your life may be, you're the asshole who made it that way.

The famous sixty hours

est is billed as "60 hours that transform your life." The course takes place over two consecutive weekends, for fifteen to eighteen hours each day, and costs three hundred dollars. Two hundred and fifty people are trained at a time. There is pretraining and posttraining at no extra charge, and for those who want to continue beyond the basic program there are ten-session evening courses for about forty-five dollars each, and other special one-day trainings.

Who goes to est?

All kinds of people. Of all ages. So far about 150,000 men and women have graduated. Most of them are enthusiastic supporters—and most of them find it difficult to put est into words. It is something one must experience, they say.

So, in describing what happens during the est training, I must make it clear that if you really want to know what est is, you must find out for yourself.

However . . .

In the beginning

On a weekday before the first weekend of the course there is a pretraining session. Attendance is not required, but it is a good idea to be there, because you will be given the ground rules for the rest of the seminars. And they are important. Actually, they aren't called "rules." They are agreements between you and the est trainers. (So, you see, already you are being made responsible for your behavior.)

Meetings are held in large, windowless rooms that can accommodate about two hundred and fifty people at a time. There will be no smoking, alcohol, marijuana, sleeping pills, uppers, downers, or any other prescription or nonprescription drugs allowed during the training, unless you have a note from your doctor. You may go to the bathroom only when the trainer says you may. You may eat only one meal and at an assigned time. There is no clock, and you must check your watch at the door. You may not sit with someone you know, and you must not talk to anyone around you while the training is being conducted. You must sit still and not move your chair or stand up unless instructed to do so. You may not leave the room for any reason unless and until you are told to do so. You must be on time and must wear your name tag at all times. If you have to eat more than once or visit the bathroom more often, or if you must take prescribed drugs or medication, you will be put in a special row in the room.

The first day

Your first day may be very uncomfortable, so be prepared for that. You may even want to leave and give up the whole idea of est. Some people do, but 99 percent of the trainees see it through.

Your trainer will lecture you for hours about your life and your mind, and why your life doesn't work. If you want to speak up or ask questions, you must use a microphone. This is called *sharing*—sharing what you think and feel—and you can say anything. The trainer makes no value judgments about either the most mundane or the most heartrending contributions. He simply acknowledges that he *got it*—he understood what you said. When you have spoken, the rest of the group will applaud.

You will hear the word *asshole* frequently—applied to you and anyone else who "gets stuck playing old mental tapes in their minds." Your chair will feel harder by the hour. You will want to go to the bathroom and you will be hungry, but you won't have any idea when you will be allowed to get relief. Without windows or a clock or your watch, you don't know what time it is. Some people will complain and be abused in return. Some will fall asleep, which is allowed. (The est people say you will benefit from the training even if you fall asleep.)

An instructor will show the group how to get rid of a headache: One must experience it, experience the pain, concentrate on its shape, color and size. Then it will disappear.

The group also will be taught how to relax: Close your eyes and concentrate on a spot in your right foot, then your left foot, and so on until you have relaxed every part of your body. While this is happening your instructor will say such phrases as "We are great," "We are all feeling good."

There are occasional rest periods, but no food may be eaten at these times. The bathroom breaks are harrowing for some, since several hundred people will be trying to use a small number of facilities in a short period of time. If you are late getting back to your seat, you'll have to accept responsibility for being late. No excuses!

Now the group is told that you all can learn to wake up at a specified time in the morning without using an alarm clock: Just visualize the process of setting the alarm—as you visualized locating specific areas of your body—and take responsibility for waking up on time.

During this very long day you are allowed only one food break, a short one, so by the time the session ends you are tired and hungry. You decide to give est another try tomorrow.

The second day

More of the same. The monotonous lectures, the restless trainees ridiculed and called assholes because they can't control their bodies. But then there is a discussion of fear, and that's different.

Fear, you are told, is not something you must try to get rid of. *Trying* to do anything is an illusion—in fact, a cop-out. Either you do something or you don't—that's being responsible. *Trying* is a way of avoiding responsibility for your life, of saying, in effect, that you don't want to do anything different with your life.

So if you are afraid of something, you must experience the fear. And when your specific fear about anything has been experienced, it will disappear.

Well, you can't help but wonder whether this is a lot of mumbo-jumbo.

Now there are more lectures, which you can barely hear, but by this time you don't care. Then, six or eight at a time, you are told to stand in a line facing—they call it *confronting*—the rest of the group. This is a fear process, and it is rough. Some people have never actually looked another human being straight in the eye. And the trainers show no mercy; they might even make fun of those in distress. Their one purpose is to assist you in getting "to the root of who you are."

One exercise almost lulls you to sleep—until the trainer tells you to visualize the people around you as your enemies. Suddenly all hell breaks loose. Some people scream and writhe on the floor, some vomit, some weep and shudder. Are they play-acting? No, they aren't. This is real. This is the direct experience of fear.

Now the trainer tells everyone in the group to close their eyes and hear the *cosmic joke:* Since each one of you has proved that you are afraid of everyone else, that means everyone else is afraid of you. Therefore, each one of you is dangerous.

This ends the second day. Believe me, by this time you are wide awake.

Midweek revelations

A curious thing is beginning to happen. As the group gathers one evening during the week to evaluate their experiences, there are fewer complaints. And there is some enthusiasm. Some people say they are communicating more effectively at home and at work. Some say they don't eat as much or go to the bathroom as often. Some are more relaxed now that they realize how foolish they were to fear the other members of the group.

You will notice, too, that the trainers are no longer calling the group members assholes. Now the assholes seem to be the non-est people.

Hey—something is happening!

The third day

You begin with a relaxation period and then go into several kinds of visualization exercises. You will learn how to build a *psychic workshop* complete with audiovisual aids and the assistance of two advisors. You can go there any time you wish and visualize yourself playing tennis or painting a picture—whatever you please—so that the next time you actually do any of these things, you will do them better.

Late at night you will be given a snack—if you can call it that. It consists of a cherry tomato, a strawberry, a daisy, a slice of lemon, a small cube of wood, and a small cube of metal. And before you can eat any of this, you must visualize yourself inside the strawberry, climbing the daisy (which you imagine to be enormous), and becoming the cubes of metal and wood. Actually, you are experiencing each of these items.

(Yes, finally you may eat the edible ones.)

More lectures. More relaxation periods. More processes—your creative imagination is working! And the third day is completed.

The fourth day

During the fourth day some people will *get it*—which is an est expression for experiencing yourself. And by experiencing, est people mean that you accept yourself exactly as you are, with no excuses. You assume complete responsibility for all of you and for all of your life.

Naturally you want to get it too. You didn't pay three hundred dollars to come away empty-handed. So you complain to the trainer that you didn't get anything yet.

This makes you an asshole again. The trainer comes right up to you and tells you you're an asshole. "Do you hear me telling you that there's nothing to get?" he shouts at you, and you feel so embarrassed that you can't say a word. You nod your head sheepishly.

"Well, then you've got it!" the trainer roars. "Sit down!"

And, of course, you do. You're confused. Again. est doesn't make sense. And yet it does.

As usual, there are lectures, but you are preoccupied with getting it. So are others in the group.

Each person who claims that he got it has a different version of what "it" is. Some say they are free from physical ailments. Some have decided to go into another line of work. Some love their spouses more, and some want a divorce. Almost all say they communicate better, have more patience, and feel in touch with themselves. To each of these definitions, the trainer simply agrees: "Then you got it."

A man grabs the microphone and says he feels cheated.

"That's what you got," the trainer smirks. "So you got it."

"I feel lousy," a woman complains.

Gradually it's coming to you. Getting it means accepting that's what you got."

"You got it," the trainer says. "That's how you feel and what you are. No matter whether it's good or bad. It simply *is*. est.

Maybe you're getting it, too. Sometimes it doesn't happen all at once.

As a graduation exercise, each member of the group does a little bit of visualization which resembles a form of ESP. He is given the name, age, and geographical location of a person he doesn't know. Only the trainer knows who it is. Then each goes into his psychic laboratory and describes the personality of this mystery person.

Amazingly, almost everyone is accurate. This is what est calls *uncovering your powers*. You weren't taught how to do this—you had it all along.

How good is est?

At a postgraduate session you will hear testimonials from many of your group members about all the problems they are now able to solve. Many will talk about their ability to accept the reality of their lives, which gives them a feeling of freedom. Without a doubt, lives are changing, decisions are being made, and, above all, the feeling that something is missing is being replaced by a feeling of getting it—whatever "it" is.

You will notice, too, that many est graduates tend to get together frequently, possibly just to share the experience of having gone through such a harrowing training. Some go back and repeat the course, for only thirty-five dollars. Some take the graduate courses. Most graduates are very evangelistic.

As for "it," well, whether you get it or not is up to you. You are responsible. And "it" for you will be different from "it" for anybody else.

Evaluating est

Of all the new therapies, mind-expansion programs, and consciousness techniques, est is by far the most controversial. Some people feel that they learned how to live by taking est, and occasionally a few are certain it didn't work. Many criticize the est methods, calling them sadistic and ridiculous. Some call them brilliant.

If you are in therapy, you must have a note from your therapist in order to take est; est is not therapy, and anyone who feels he is on the edge, or who specifically wants therapy, should go to a therapist, not to est.

est is an education. As I say, I'm biased, and I feel est is probably the education every one of us could have benefited from long, long ago. It is what is really going on inside us behind the mask we wear to face the world, and even behind the second mask we wear to face ourselves.

Behind all that is what est calls the Self, not to be confused with the ego. The Self is the essence inside each of us. It is where the love is, and that is the same for each of us. Going through the barriers of the layers of personality frees many est graduates in many ways to live more responsibly, more spontaneously, more lovingly.

CHAPTER 22
HOW TO CHOOSE A THERAPIST

As this book is being written, there are 130 different kinds of therapies and self-improvement techniques available to help you solve your problems, develop your potential, expand your mind, express yourself effectively, and get more satisfaction out of life. In the field of psychotherapy alone, there are 30 different versions of treatment. If you were to take another count in a month from now, I'm sure there would be more.

Assuming that you already know how some of these programs differ from others, and which is right for you, you still have an important decision to make: choosing your therapist. This is the person who will guide you along the path to getting better, and the relationship between the two of you can make the difference between success and failure.

In fact, many therapists feel that the person you work with is more important than the kind of therapy she practices.

That makes sense, doesn't it? After all, whether you are in psychoanalytic therapy or biofeedback or Arica training or est, your therapist, guide, instructor, or whatever you want to call her, becomes the most influential person in your life. At least for a time. And perhaps for the rest of your life, when you consider the results of your training or therapy.

A therapist should be someone you can trust. Someone you can talk to. Someone who can share your pain and anticipate your joys. Someone who is strong enough to resist your attempts to manipulate, yet can gently draw you out of your shell. Someone who will respect your privacy and who you know won't go around telling others about your innermost thoughts and feelings. Someone who will give part of herself to your relationship, who relates to you as another human being and not as a judge or an authority. Someone who understands what it means to want to be more, do more, have more, and give more.

That's a tall order. Such persons aren't easy to find. But they do exist. And they are worth searching for.

Where?

Therapists come in all sizes, all ages, both sexes, and all sexual preferences. They have different kinds of training, different personal backgrounds; they come from different cultural environments, and their personalities certainly are different.

So how do you find one?

By asking.

Ask your friends, especially those who have worked with a therapist and who seem to have benefited from it.

Ask your doctor or your clergyman.

Call your community mental health center and ask for a list of therapists in your area.

Call your nearest teaching hospital and ask for referrals. Also call your nearest medical school.

Call your county mental health association (listed under "Mental Health Association of ______").

Look in the white pages of the telephone book for hot-line numbers under headings such as "alcoholism," "drug abuse," etc.

Training

There are licensed and unlicensed therapists, but don't assume that a license always makes the difference between a competent and an incompentent practitioner. It doesn't. Some therapies require licensing and some don't. Just be sure that your therapist is licensed if his therapy requires it. And licensing usually is an additional verification of general competence.

The training of therapists differs according to the therapy. The following guidelines will help you determine whether your therapist is qualified to practice what he preaches:

Psychiatrists are medical doctors who have also completed three years of psychiatric residency in addition to their medical internship. Some are psychoanalytically trained (they have been through a personal analysis as well), and all may prescribe drugs. Recommended are those who have a state license, and are either certified by the American Board of Psychiatry and Neurology or are "board eligible."

Psychologists are not medical doctors. They have at least a master's degree, and some have a Ph. D. Some treat patients. Some perform tests or conduct research. Recommended are those with a state license and certification by the American Board of Examiners in Professional Psychology or listing in the National Register of Health Service Providers in Psychology.

Social workers often are associated with hospitals and clinics, and do have private practices as well, but their training in therapy techniques can be similar to that of psychologists and psychiatrists. Recommended are those with at least a master's degree (MSW or MSSW) and accreditation by the Academy of Certified Social Workers.

Psychoanalysts usually are either psychiatrists or psychologists, but not necessarily so. The only required training is in the technique of psychoanalysis itself, and in some states there is specific accreditation. Sometimes a person becomes a psychoanalyst if she masters the technique, and sometimes there are objective criteria as to whether or not such mastery is sufficient for successful therapy.

Pastoral counselors are clergy who may or may not be trained in psychology or sociology. Recommended are those with degrees in these studies.

Paraprofessionals practice limited forms of therapy and do not have enough training to qualify for a degree in any specialty. They are not licensed or accredited. Recommended are those who have completed two years of training that qualifies them to be called "mental health assistant," "psychiatric counselor," "activity therapist," or "nurse's aide."

The therapist as a person

No matter how well trained a therapist is, he may not be the right one for you. He may have done wonders for your friend, but that doesn't mean he will get the same results with you.

Why not?

Well, for one thing, you're a human being and so is he. Your personalities may not feel right intuitively. You may not communicate well with each other. Clashing, arguing may not be a sign that the therapist is wrong. For you, conversely, it may be right.

But suppose, for instance, that you're a very casual person. You wear your hair in a natural style, you're comfortable in jeans, and your language is earthy. You may not feel comfortable talking to a therapist who wears his hair short on the sides and walks around in wing-tip shoes. Or maybe that's just what you're looking for and you're disappointed because your therapist shows up in jeans more faded than yours.

You may not like someone whose grammar is flawless—or you may hate slang. A therapist who comes on as friendly may help you to open up—or may make you withdraw in suspicion. Or your homosexuality may send you to a homosexual therapist.

Your preferences aren't silly, and you should take them seriously. They influence your ability to communicate and be communicated with. And communication is the keystone to any form of therapy.

Getting to know your therapist

You really ought to shop around for a therapist. Shop until you find one who makes you feel comfortable, someone you feel will listen when you talk, and someone who gives you the feeling that you want to listen when *she* talks.

How?

Start with your telephone. You can't always dial the therapist's number and get her on the phone. But you can tell her secretary or answering service that you would like to talk to her and leave your number.

When you talk to a therapist, be ready with a list of written questions next to the phone:

Can she see you soon? Some therapists are booked up for months and perhaps you don't want to wait that long.

How much does she charge?

How long is a therapeutic session?

The next question you may have to ask in person:

What kind of therapeutic techniques does she use and how will you benefit from them? This is not an evaluation you want—and you shouldn't be asking for such a thing at this point. You simply want to know what you will get out of therapy.

By the time you run through these questions, you and the therapist should have some idea of how well you are communicating with each other and whether you are comfortable with each other. If things feel right, the next step is to make an appointment to see the therapist. Naturally, that will cost you money, but it will cost the therapist the investment of her professional time—and fair is fair.

As you talk to the therapist you will have more questions, and don't be shy about asking them. After a few sessions she should be able to tell you what your needs are and how her form of therapy can fulfill them. She also should be able to tell you *approximately* how long you will have to be in therapy to reach your goals. You have a right to know what your therapy will cost in terms of time and money.

If you plan to go into a group type of program, you still ought to shop around. How you feel about your instructor or therapist is just as important as if you were on a one-to-one basis with her.

If you're going into group psychotherapy, use the same approach you would use going into individual therapy. But if you're going into something like a TA course or yoga classes, go to one of the introductory sessions (which, incidentally, might be free). Don't be content to listen to the lectures and read the pamphlets—go up and speak to the instructors. Ask them how they think their program will help you. Give yourself a chance to find out whether you and the therapists are comfortable with each other.

If you're short of money, that doesn't rule out therapy for you. Some programs, such as Arica training, offer scholarships for those who can't afford their usual fees. Then there are clinics associated with hospitals, medical schools, and mental health centers. Here, too, you still have a choice. You don't have to work with the therapist assigned to you. You can say, "No, thank you very much, but I need to feel more of a rapport with a therapist."

Remember this: A good therapist will not take your rejection personally. She should know—better than you—that the ability of the patient and therapist to work well together is half the therapy.

Are you getting better?

How will you know your therapy is successful?

Because you look forward to it all day or all week? Because you feel better, happier, more alive? Because your therapist tells you so?

No.

You may not always look forward to your session with your therapist. At times you may dread it, especially when your defenses are crumbling and your carefully withheld real self is about to emerge. In fact, in many instances the more progress you make, the more uncomfortable you may feel, simply because you are letting go of your old way of life and you don't know what to expect from the new.

Simply being in therapy may make you happier. After all, you're getting some attention, and that makes anyone feel better. For a while. It doesn't necessarily mean you're making progress.

Chances are your therapist won't tell you how you're doing. He wants *you* to tell *him*.

So the best gauge of the success of your therapy is you in your daily life. If you notice that you're changing, that you seem happier, more relaxed, that you're able to handle your problems without going to pieces or leaning on others, that you're easier to talk to, more sensitive to the feelings of others, that you're able to express your feelings, that you can make decisions and seem to know where you're going—then that's a good indication that your therapy is working.

And if it isn't?

Every therapy has its good and bad times, and if you're having a bad time you should wait before deciding to change therapists. The trouble may not be your therapist at all. It may be you. If so, this is something that should come out in the course of your therapy.

But if, after a reasonable time, you still feel stuck, if you're still wrestling with the same problems you brought with you into therapy, if those who live and work with you see no change—or a change for the worse—then you are correct to think about changing your therapist. And I can't tell you what a "reasonable" time is; you'll have to decide.

If you are unsure about your progress, you can ask for a

consultation with another therapist. There is no reason why your therapist should object to this request, because he should be just as troubled by your lack of progress as you are. A third party may be able to point out obstacles to your communication which, when removed, will enable you and your therapist to work together very well. Or the third party may suggest that you part company.

When you get better

Some people are reluctant to go into any form of therapy because they think it has to last forever.

It certainly doesn't!

But don't expect your therapist to tell you when to end it. That's up to you. Ending it is part of the therapy.

Perhaps you'll feel that you're able to go on your way by yourself—but you'll have a few doubts. In that case, you can arrange to check back with your therapist from time to time. If you run into problems you can't handle, you can always go back into therapy.

If you're in a program such as assertiveness training or est, you may want to repeat the course or go on to graduate courses because you feel the repetition gives you added value. That's fine. But, even so, the time will come when you'll feel that you have learned enough to depend on yourself.

Fine.

Because getting better means good-bye. And hello.

Part 2
Diagnosing Yourself

CHAPTER 23 WHAT'S YOUR PROBLEM?

Now that you have a better understanding of the most widely available therapies and techniques to help you get more *ah-h-h-h!* out of your life, your next step is to find out what is causing your dissatisfaction. Then you can select the therapy or technique—or both—best suited to help you deal with it.

In the following twelve sections you will read about problems common to our culture. Included in each section will be descriptions of symptoms typical of a problem, some warning signals that such a problem may be developing, and a list of treatments generally considered to be effective in relation to it.

But—I know what you're going to say—why only *twelve* problems? Surely there are more?

Quite true. Almost as many problems as there are people. And if we were to deal with each one, we would run out of paper. So, to make things easier, I have selected what I consider to be the twelve most common problems of our time.

Just as in narrowing down the choices of therapies to be included in this book, the final selection of problems is—and must be, in all honesty—a subjective one. These are the problems *I* find to be most evident. They are the ones about which most people talk to me, the ones I see most often around me in my work and my life. They also are the problems several of my colleagues listed when I conferred with them. In short, in my opinion—and in the opinion of several associates in my field—these twelve problems are the ones that are troubling most people most of the time.

You will find several therapies and techniques matched up

with each problem, and the final choice is up to you. You now know quite a bit about how each therapy works, so choose the one—or ones—that will work best for you. Remember, that's why there are so many different ways of getting better. Take your own personality needs into consideration.

Again, I have to allow est to stand by itself, because while est is not a problem-solving technique, it does seem to have an effect on the problems of those who complete the training. (See Chapter 21 for a more detailed explanation.) For this reason I have recommended est for all the problems.

THE PROBLEM: ADDICTION

For Example:

A twenty-eight-year-old woman pops pills to forget the pain of feeling unacceptable. Occasionally she can break the habit—until something goes wrong. A broken romance, an argument with her parents, a disappointing vacation—and she's back on drugs. Even when things are going well, she keeps her supply of drugs around, just in case.

A successful, middle-aged black lawyer drinks too much because he can't deal with the memories of his childhood. He was born in a ghetto, one of ten children in a poor family, and although he worked his way up in the world he still feels somewhat unworthy and alienated. His wife is worried about him; she knows he's an alcoholic.

A seriously overweight young woman eats too much and can't stay on a diet. Her weight depresses her, which causes her to eat even more. It all started when she was a child and her adoring parents showered her with edible goodies as a gesture of affection. She was an overweight child and an object of ridicule in school, a problem her parents attempted to allay by offering still more food to soothe the pain. Recently the young woman's mother died, and the girl has been on an eating binge that is threatening her health.

A thirty-year-old man has been a compulsive gambler since he was a teenager. When he wins he lives in a dream world of luxury and big spending, but when he's on a losing streak he's not only broke but frightened. Sometimes he borrows money from loansharks, and he isn't sure he can pay it back. He'd like to stop gambling, but it's the only way he feels important, and then only when he wins.

Warning Signals:

There are many kinds of addiction, but here we will consider four very common ones.

About drugs:

You can't admit to yourself, or anyone else, the amount of drugs you're taking.

You hoard prescriptions, renewing them before they are used up.

You remain on diet drugs after you've lost weight.

You take sleeping pills regularly, not only when you can't sleep.

Your supply—and how to get it—is becoming the most important thing in your life.

About drinking:

You save empty liquor bottles.

You drink when you're alone.

You drink to avoid pain.

You drink when you have problems.

You're always thinking about the next drink; in fact, time is beginning to tick from drink to drink.

About overeating:

You lie about the amount you eat.

You sneak food when no one is around.

You eat when you have problems, when you're under pressure or depressed.

About gambling:

Winning makes you feel like a big shot.

You can't stick to your limit, even when you're losing.

You can't quit when you're ahead.

You sometimes gamble with money you need for rent, mortgage, food.

You borrow money, often at high interest rates, to gamble.

Here's Help:

Support group therapy (such as Alcoholics Anonymous) for peer acceptance, encouragement, recognition of the problem.

Psychoanalytic therapy for uncovering the unconscious motivation from early life.

Transactional analysis for a self-regulatory system and strengthening the Adult ego state.

Bioenergetics and Gestalt for awareness of the problem and conscious expression of feelings related to it.

Transcendental meditation for relaxation techniques, relief from stress.

Silva Mind Control for relaxation of tension, physical rehabilitation, visualized healing.

est.

Behavior modification to recondition responses to stimuli.

Hypnosis, especially posthypnotic suggestion, to suppress the addiction.

THE PROBLEM: CAN'T MAKE DECISIONS

For Example:

An extremely beautiful sportswear designer in her early thirties is having affairs with several men simultaneously. Each man wants to live with her or marry her, and she says she feels ready for a deeper, one-to-one relationship now. But she can't decide which of her lovers she wants for a long-term commitment, because she's afraid the one she chooses may turn out to be the wrong man for her. Actually, she is avoiding taking responsibility for herself, and eventually she will allow the men in her life to make the decision for her by becoming impatient and walking out.

A bookkeeper in his early forties has been passed over for promotion since his rival became head of his department. He notices that he is no longer included in important meetings and conferences. He knows he should begin to look around for a new job, but he is afraid he will have difficulty because of his age. He also doesn't want to give up the pension and profit-sharing benefits of his present job. So he keeps writing résumés and throwing them in the wastebasket. He is so preoccupied with making a decision that his work is beginning to suffer, making his job situation more precarious.

Warning Signals:

You don't want to give up any alternatives, so you try to hold on to them for as long as you can.

When you're able to make a decision, you can't act on it.

You feel there is too much responsibility involved in making a decision.

Your head tells you one thing and your heart tells you another.

You're afraid that once you make a decision, you won't be able to change it.

You wish someone else would tell you what to do.

Here's Help:

Psychoanalytic therapy (individual and group), transactional analysis for exploring the underlying motivations and increasing an awareness of the reality consequences of decisions.

Gestalt, Silva Mind Control, transcendental meditation, Arica training, yoga for increased intuitiveness, sensitivity to new options, and learning to induce a relaxed state of mind when making decisions.

Assertiveness training for learning how to carry out decisions once you have made them.

est.

THE PROBLEM: DEPRESSION

For Example:

An eighteen-year-old girl, the youngest in a family of five children, and usually a cheerful, outgoing person, has been behaving strangely. She began attending college almost a year ago but had to drop out and return home because she was miserable in the new environment and was unable to make friends among the other students. Since she is home she seems to have lost interest in everything except her guitar, which she plays by the hour. She doesn't seek out her friends, doesn't want to continue her education, and feels she isn't qualified to look for a job. Her appetite, which used to be excellent, is so poor that she is alarmingly thin, and she doesn't sleep well. She cries all night long, but doesn't know why.

A young draftsman is very close to losing his job because he comes to work half stoned on pot almost every day. He is exceptionally bright but doesn't make the best use of his abilities, because he is afraid to compete with his father, whom he considers brilliant. In fact, he does as little as possible and makes no effort to have a relationship with anyone. In conversation he has to be drawn out, and answers, maddeningly, in monosyllables. He uses drugs to avoid the depressing conviction that he is going to die soon.

Warning Signals:

You can't sleep well—or you sleep most of the time.

You lost your appetite—or you're eating much more than you should.

You don't have any energy.

You cry often and for long periods of time, but without relief.

You've been sad for a long time, and apparently without reason.

You're pessimistic, hopeless, and feel life isn't worth living.

You have trouble concentrating.

You don't want to see your friends anymore, and you've lost interest in your work.

You can't seem to have fun anymore.

Sometimes you think about suicide.

You were terribly depressed by the death of someone close to you, but that was several months ago and you still feel the same.

Here's Help:

Note: Since depression usually is caused by unexpressed anger that is turned in upon the self, the following methods are recommended for dealing with that anger.

Psychoanalytic therapy (individual and group) and transactional analysis for getting at a deeply rooted, complex anger and its roots in the past.

Gestalt and bioenergetics for uncovering less complicated anger and facilitating its expression.

Assertiveness training for learning new ways to deal with anger.

est, while not attempting to solve the problem of depression, does seem to enable a more direct expression of all emotions.

THE PROBLEM: INFERIORITY FEELINGS

For Example:

A quiet thirty-five-year-old man acts like a dummy, yet tests out as quite intelligent. He drifts from job to job, never doing anything meaningful. He lives in a furnished room, which he does nothing to improve, and has friends who take advantage of his patience, his generosity, and his unending willingness to help them solve their problems. As a child he was overprotected and smothered by his mother, who always held him back, and by the time he went to school he was convinced he couldn't measure up to other children. His mother's anxiety about his health, strength, and safety made him afraid to try anything for fear he would fail. Now he is so convinced of his inadequacy that he finds ways to prove to himself that he really is inferior. For instance, when a family in his neighborhood invited him to dinner, he got the date all mixed up and arrived two days late. He wasn't invited again, which deprived him of an opportunity to form a relationship with people who were genuinely interested in him.

A young man with a great deal of talent as an artist has been working in the art department of a magazine for several years without getting the recognition he deserves. He allows his boss to take credit for his innovative ideas and does not attempt to have himself included in meetings at which new layouts and illustrations are planned. He says he would feel nervous speaking in a roomful of people. He also is reluctant to ask for a raise, even though he hasn't had one for a long time, and feels that if his work really were worth more money, he would be getting it. On his walls at home are excellent watercolors he has painted, but they are exhibited only because his wife thinks they are beautiful. Whenever anyone admires them, the young man shrugs his shoulders and says they really aren't very good but it was nice of the person to say so.

Warning Signals:

You put yourself down at every opportunity.

You refuse compliments when they are given.

You solicit compliments if they aren't given.

You're afraid to try anything because you think you'll fail—and if you don't try, then you can't fail.

You're afraid to say no for fear of being rejected.

You feel as if other people are adults and you're a child.

You don't feel strong enough to compete with anyone.

You allow your friends to step all over you.

Here's Help:

Psychoanalytic therapy for understanding unconscious fears.

Transactional analysis for a system of strengthening the Adult and Child ego states and giving you permission to be who you are.

Behavior modification, especially if the inferiority feeling is related to something specific, such as an authority figure or an audience.

Assertiveness training for teaching you how to get what you want.

est.

Gestalt for putting you in touch with your unexpressed aggression.

Primal Therapy for severe, chronic feelings of inferiority that do not respond to other forms of treatment.

Silva Mind Control and transcendental meditation to build a sense of self-esteem.

Sex therapy when feelings of inadequacy are related to sexual expression.

Group psychotherapy and encounter groups when inferiority feelings handicap social life.

Rolfing for self-confidence based on improved flow of body energy.

Bioenergetics for uncovering repressed emotions and building confidence through physical fitness.

THE PROBLEM: INSOMNIA

For Example:

A little boy whose parents constantly warned him not to sin because God would punish him severely if he did has now grown into a young man who cannot sleep. He is afraid that if he falls asleep, all kinds of terrible things will happen: He will die, or someone will break into his house and harm him. His insomnia is such a handicap that the young man must continue to live with his parents, and recently turned down an offer of a better job because it would have meant moving away.

Warning Signals:

You stay awake at night because you're afraid of the dark or your dreams.

You stay awake because you're afraid of dying in your sleep, or you think an intruder will break in and harm you.

You can't sleep at night long after you have recovered from a period of anxiety.

You've solved your problems, but you still can't sleep.

You take pills to induce sleep.

You become hyperactive around bedtime.

You lie awake worrying about approaching deadlines or unfinished work.

Here's Help:

Psychoanalytic therapy for exploring the unconscious basis of your fears.

Transcendental meditation for all aspects of insomnia and, in cases of tension, for relaxation techniques.

Behavior modification, especially when insomnia is fear-related, for reconditioning responses to fearful thoughts. Also for relaxation techniques.

est.

Gestalt for uncovering unexpressed emotions such as anger, fear, guilt, etc.

Primal Therapy for the release of lifelong fears which do not yield to other approaches.

Hypnosis for posthypnotic and autohypnotic suggestions to sleep.

Silva Mind Control, biofeedback, Arica training, and yoga for relaxation techniques and self-inducement of sleep, especially if insomnia is mild.

THE PROBLEM: MAINTAINING RELATIONSHIPS

For Example:

A woman in her late thirties has been married to her childhood sweetheart since she was seventeen. The couple have four children, only one of whom is still at home. Both the husband and wife dropped out of high school when they married, and their lack of training has made it very difficult for either of them to find a well-paying job. She solicits insurance by telephone and has worked most of the time since she was married. Her husband is a gas station attendant when he can find work, which is not often. Their marriage has always been troubled by money problems, which cause frequent and bitter arguments. And when it isn't money, some other crisis seems to take its place. There has never been a time of quiet and peace. When the woman's resentment toward her husband becomes too much for her, she gets drunk. In reprisal, her husband stays away for several days, often with another woman.

Some of the woman's friends have urged her to end the marriage, especially now that her children are grown, but she says she doesn't want to leave her husband because they have been through so much together. The marriage counselor she and her husband are consulting has pointed out to the couple that they really do not have an intimate relationship in spite of the years they have been together. Their lives just seem to go from crisis to crisis, with no space between in which the two might get to know and understand each other better. The counselor also has made the wife aware that she contributes to her husband's immaturity by taking too many responsibilities upon herself. What this couple needs is a greater sensitivity to their own and each other's needs.

A young man in medical school makes friends easily but can't hold on to them. He is an extremely obliging person, which attracts people to him, has a good sense of humor, and likes to put ideas into action, which makes him a popular leader. Before long, however, he begins to feel that his friends take advantage of his good disposition and show no consideration for his needs. He is convinced they like him only for the favors he can do and not for what he is. For instance, when he came close to failing one of his courses, no one offered him encouragement or help. No one seemed to realize that beneath his usual smile he was scared stiff. Gradually the young man will withdraw from his friendships and probably he will transfer to another medical school next year—where he will try again to make more-lasting relationships.

Warning Signals:

Your relationships get off to an exciting start, but they soon bog down in boredom.

You're really more comfortable alone than with others.

People always disappoint you by not living up to all you see in them.

You do the giving and others do the taking—or so it seems.

You don't like anyone to get too close to you.

You can't tell a friend, lover, or spouse how you really feel.

You're sure that if you could just meet the right person, all your problems would be solved.

You find it very hard to give up what you want to do in favor of someone else's preferences.

You're shocked when people close to you say you're insensitive, and you can't understand how you're expected to know how they feel.

Here's Help:

est.

Psychoanalytic therapy for understanding how present relationships are influenced by those in the past.

Transactional analysis for clarifying your present needs and learning to communicate them.

Behavior modification to reduce anxiety and recondition the way you respond to others.

Assertiveness training for learning how to say no without ending a relationship.

Gestalt for an awareness of areas of immaturity.

Marriage groups for an understanding of intimacy.

Group therapy for understanding how you interact with others.

Silva Mind Control for developing self-esteem.

Sex therapy for improving communication of sexual needs.

Bioenergetics for deeper self-knowledge, awareness and communication of needs.

THE PROBLEM: NEED TO GROW

For Example:

A fifty-year-old woman wonders why she feels so restless lately. She is a doctor in private practice and enjoys her work, but she wishes she could devote some of her professional time to research. Her marriage is good and her husband has always encouraged her to grow and develop herself. She and her children are friends, and she delights in being a grandmother. But she senses the need for something more challenging in life.

Every once in a while a thirty-two-year-old college English instructor indulges his favorite fantasy. He sees himself saying good-bye to his students, getting in his car, and going off to a small cabin on the edge of a lake high up in the mountains, where he begins work on a book he wants to write. But the fantasy is always interrupted by a student who needs help, an associate who wants to know if the instructor can take over his class the next day, or one of the many other practical demands of making a living. While the instructor isn't exactly unhappy with his life, he feels he is stagnating. Perhaps, he thinks, he should stop telling his students how to write and get down to writing itself. Something in him wants to be expressed and, at times, when he seems preoccupied, he is wondering what it might be.

A young mother of three small children used to be quite satisfied with her life. She had grown up in a small town in a depressed area of the country where jobs were scarce and every penny had to be stretched. She left home and found work in a large Midwestern city, where she met and married a young man whose family owned a large, successful construction company. Suddenly the young woman didn't have to worry about money or security. She lived in a spacious house in an attractive neighborhood and drove her own car. She could afford whatever she needed. As soon as she became pregnant she gave up her job, which she never had liked, and was content to be at home with her growing family.

Now, however, she is beginning to resent her husband's opportunities to meet interesting people, discuss ideas, and, especially, be completely absorbed in his work. The young woman feels deprived, especially when she reads about some single young women who seem to have very exciting lives. She wants the freedom to travel, to go to parties and unusual restaurants, to meet glamorous people, take courses that interest her, and try different lifestyles. She was beginning to blame her husband for tying her down, and one day it all came out in an argument. Much to her surprise, she discovered that her husband could understand how she felt once she made her feelings clear. She realized also that he is not the cause of her problem. *She* is. She envied single women because they seemed to have no responsibilities, but of course that wasn't true and she knows it now. Her marriage allows her plenty of room to expand, but whether she does it—and how—is up to her.

Warning Signals:

You're wondering who you really are.
You ask yourself what you want out of life.

You want to know the meaning of life.

Your life seems empty in spite of the fact that you "have everything."

You want more-meaningful relationships.

You sense some undeveloped potential within yourself.

You notice that your body is out of tone and less flexible than it should be.

Your mind needs a challenge.

You realize there are so many unexplored paths in your life, and you wonder where they might lead.

Here's Help:

est for getting at the fundamental experience of experience.

Transcendental meditation for spiritual fulfillment, mental development, and awareness of cosmic forces.

Gestalt for increased awareness of where you are right now.

Transactional analysis for increased awareness of the self in relationship to others.

Silva Mind Control for increased sensitivity to your own needs and those of others.

Arica training for deeper understanding of the self in relation to the environment, and for psychic sensitization.

Bioenergetics for discovering and removing unconscious blocks to growth.

Yoga for development and integration of body, mind, and spirit.

Sex therapy for making good sex even better through an understanding of needs and sensory-awareness techniques.

Rolfing for freeing and redirecting body energy.

Group psychotherapy for improving relationships.

Marriage encounter groups for restoring intimacy and improving communication.

THE PROBLEM: PHOBIAS

For Example:

An attractive middle-aged woman is so afraid to go up or down stairs that she must plan every event in her life with great care. She and her husband live in a one-story home and she has never been down to the basement or up to the attic. When they go out to dinner, they go to a restaurant that has no stairs between the entrance and the dining room. The woman cannot visit friends in houses that are not on street level. She cannot work in a building where she must use stairs to get in and out. If she is somehow forced by circumstances to go up or down stairs, she becomes hysterical.

Warning Signals:

You're afraid of a specific thing, person, or place.

When you approach the thing you fear, you have an intense desire to run away from it.

You're afraid that whatever you fear might cause you to hurt yourself, such as by jumping off a high mountain.

You're afraid that the thing you fear might cause you to hurt someone else, such as by shooting someone with a gun.

You plan your life around avoiding what you fear.

Here's Help:

Psychoanalytic therapy to get at the underlying meaning of your anxiety and its relationship to early life.

Transactional analysis for understanding and changing the ego states associated with your anxiety.

Gestalt if the problem seems to be related to unexpressed emotions, especially anger.

est.

Bioenergetics to uncover the cause of the anxiety and gain mastery over it.

Behavior modification for relaxation techniques, an understanding of the way the phobia has conditioned your behavior, and reconditioning the responses to whatever causes your anxiety.

Transcendental meditation, yoga, biofeedback for inducing relaxation to ease the stress in mild phobias.

THE PROBLEM: SEX

For Example:

An attractive young man with very little sex experience is meeting with one failure after another. He is convinced that other men do not have this problem and that superb lovemaking comes naturally and easily to them. He also is so afraid that he will not be able to help a woman achieve an orgasm that he is unable to have one himself. A physical examination revealed nothing functionally wrong, yet the problem continues, because it is rooted in the young man's fear of being found sexually inadequate. (This, incidentally, is the most common sex problem among men.)

A thirty-year-old woman has always accepted the fact that she is frigid, because she rarely has an orgasm. She is married, had premarital sex experience, and enjoys her sex life, but feels self-conscious about her inability to climax. Recently she was surprised to read that the word *frigid* is an inaccurate description of her condition. The correct term is *preorgasmic*, because unless there is something physically wrong, every woman can have an orgasm—in fact, one after another. Many women just don't know *how*.

A man in his mid-thirties whose wife has gone back to school for a graduate degree has been troubled lately by premature ejaculation. The harder he tries to hold back, the more quickly he climaxes, which is so frustrating that sometimes he sits up watching TV, waiting for his wife to fall asleep before he goes to bed. What he cannot admit to himself is the fact that he looks upon his wife's resumption of her education as a threat to him and a form of neglect of his own needs. His premature ejaculation may very well be his way of getting back at her, as if he were withholding something (satisfaction) from her.

A middle-aged woman, widowed for two years, feels guilty about masturbating. She reads a great deal about the subject and would like to believe that there isn't any harm in it, but in her childhood she was taught that masturbation was an unhealthy perversion and she can't forget that. Her real problem, however, is that although she masturbates several times a day, she gets no sexual satisfaction from it. She also avoids any possibility of a sexual relationship with someone else.

Warning Signals:

You're afraid you won't satisfy your sex partner.

You can't let yourself go when you're making love.

You're ashamed of your body.

You're afraid you're impotent or preorgasmic, but you don't know what the words really mean.

You're afraid to have a physical examination.

You blame your partner for your lack of sexual satisfaction.

Sex makes you feel guilty.

Your sex fantasies make you uncomfortable.

You can't express your own sexual needs or ask about your partner's.

You can't talk about sex without feeling embarrassed.

Here's Help:

est.

Psychoanalytic therapy for an understanding of past influences on present attitudes.

Transactional analysis for strengthening your OK Child and decreasing the influence of your Not-OK Parent.

Marriage group for improving communication.

Bioenergetics for release of blocks to sexual expression.

Behavior modification for learning new ways to respond.

Gestalt for understanding how you are distorting reality.

Sex therapy for direct retraining of the sexual response, relaxation techniques, and an understanding of your body.

Transcendental meditation for alert relaxation to reduce anxiety.

Silva Mind Control for increased awareness of movement and relaxation techniques.

Rolfing for release of physical tension.

Yoga for increased mental awareness, physical flexibility, relaxation.

Arica training for freedom from intruding thoughts.

THE PROBLEM: STUCK IN THE PAST

For Example:

A woman whose parents cruelly abused her as a child is reliving the pattern over and over in the present. She has been married twice, both times unsuccessfully and both times to men who beat her—although she repeatedly courted their rage with her infidelity. Even now she cannot relate to supportive, genuinely affectionate people, partly because she is afraid they will turn on her and partly because she has a compulsion to reexperience the intensity of the brutal events of her childhood. In a sense she is trying to go back to her past and gain control over the traumatic events, but she ends up being trapped in a repetition of past misery.

A forty-year-old man who had an especially happy youth is still trying to relive his high-school days. He wears his old school sweater every chance he gets, loves to reread his yearbook (which he keeps on the coffee table), and sings the school songs in the shower. At parties and even at business lunches he bores people by repeating the same tired stories about his high-school days. He has no interest in the present and very little awareness of what is going on in the world.

Warning Signals:

You deliberately behave in ways that are different from those in your past. (Because you want to avoid the powerful grip your past has on you.)

You try to do everything just as you did it years ago.

You can't remember much about your past—or you remember in great detail.

You find yourself describing the same past events over and over.

You feel haunted by something that happened long ago.

You're convinced that the best part of your life is over.

You're not interested in present events.

Here's Help:

Gestalt and Primal Therapy for uncovering and releasing painful past events.

Hypnosis for putting you in touch with a forgotten traumatic experience.

Group therapy for understanding the past and moving on to the future.

Behavior modification for deconditioning self-defeating responses learned in the past, desensitizing responses to present anxiety, and learning new ways to respond to present situations.

Psychoanalytic therapy and transactional analysis for understanding how past events influence present behavior.

Bioenergetics and Rolfing for unlocking bodily pain caused

by past experiences, and enabling a more direct expression of those feelings.

est.

THE PROBLEM: TENSION

For Example:

A production manager for a publishing company has been told by his doctor that he has high blood pressure and must find a way to reduce the stress in his life. His job carries a lot of responsibility and he is constantly caught up in a struggle to meet the editors' demands for handsome books and the treasurer's insistence on reduced production costs. He is unable to confront either side with the fact that their demands are often conflicting and that they must sometimes choose between economy and beauty.

The strain of this man's predicament is affecting his health. He suffers painful indigestion after his meals, and he is afraid he is developing ulcers. At night, when he goes home, he is so wound up that he has one drink after another, trying to relax but becoming depressed instead. In the wee hours he begins calling up his friends, waking them from sleep and telling them about his troubles until either they become impatient and hang up or he begins to sob uncontrollably. Now that his doctor has warned him, he feels more tense than ever. He knows he could never just go off on vacation and leave his worries behind. Frankly, he is scared.

A thirty-five-year-old woman has just been hospitalized for colitis for the third time in two years. Her doctor says her illness is caused by family tensions, which she says is ridiculous—she has a very happy family. She cannot admit to herself that she has repressed her resentment toward her husband and children to such a degree that she is almost physically incapable of living with them. On the surface she is the doting mother and devoted wife who gives all and asks nothing for herself. Her problem is that she *cannot* ask for anything she needs, wants, or prefers, but expects her husband and children to sense her yearning intuitively and give her *something*—attention, perhaps a little gift, a bit of their time. So on and on she goes, playing the martyr and raging inside, until finally the strain brings on such unbearable physical pain that she must be hospitalized.

Warning Signals:

You feel as if you are being pulled in two opposite directions.

You avoid conflict and confrontation.

You hold back your anger, even when it seems justified.

No matter how hard you try, you can't relax.

Your muscles feel rigid and your body aches all over.

You're always tired, even after a good sleep.

You've been told that your high blood pressure, ulcers, or indigestion is caused by stress.

You feel so edgy that you're beginning to avoid people.

Sometimes you explode with anger at the slightest provocation.

Here's Help:

Transactional analysis, psychoanalytic therapy, Gestalt for getting at the fundamental causes of tension.

Primal Therapy for uncovering especially painful causes, and for early relief when the emotions are rubbed raw.

Hypnosis for releasing pent-up feelings caused by trauma early in life.

Assertiveness training for overcoming tension caused by being a pushover.

est.

Bioenergetics for getting at and releasing repressed emotions.

Behavior modification for desensitizing responses to anxiety, and for relaxation techniques.

Silva Mind Control, transcendental meditation, biofeedback, and yoga for relaxation of mind and body, plus prevention of tension.

Rolfing for freeing the body from distortions caused by tension.

THE PROBLEM: UNCONTROLLABLE EMOTIONS

For Example:

A young nurse who is usually very calm and efficient lately had caused concern among the other members of the hospital staff because she will, without warning, erupt with anger for no apparent reason. It doesn't happen often, but when it does its unsettling. The young woman is quite steady in the face of pain, suffering, and death, but one day, when she came into the nurses' lounge and found the coffeepot empty, she swore and smashed the pot against the wall. Another time she found some linens stored on the wrong shelf in a closet and angrily pulled them off, leaving them in a heap on the floor.

A young salesman is having a difficult time meeting his quotas because he laughs too easily, and for no apparent reason, when talking to his customers. He realizes it is a form of nervousness, but he just can't seem to control himself, and the more embarrassed he feels, the more he laughs. It's become a vicious cycle which is leading to an almost paralyzing inability to function on the job.

A wife and mother of two small children finds that she has spells of crying that may last for hours. She can't think of anything specific that would cause her to feel so depressed, but the crying spells are occurring more frequently. She knows she is very tired, and she wishes she could talk to her husband about getting away for a vacation, but she finds it very hard to express herself to him. He is working hard trying to get ahead, and she doesn't want to add to his problems. In fact, she tries to be cheerful for him even when she isn't happy. Sometimes she feels like a volcano about to erupt.

Warning Signals:

You feel guilty about being angry, disappointed, sad, or anxious.

You start laughing over something funny and can't stop, or you cry for a good reason and can't stop.

You feel an emotion building up in you and you're afraid of what will happen if you can't keep it in.

Here's Help:

Psychoanalytic therapy, transactional analysis, and group therapy for an understanding of how the ego states regulate emotions and how to strengthen or loosen their control.

Assertiveness training to strengthen your ability to express your feelings directly and in proportion to the situation.

Gestalt and bioenergetics for uncovering repressed feelings and facilitating their expression.

Primal Therapy when feelings are especially painful.

est.

Let's Not Forget the Human Problem

As you read through these problems, did you begin to see yourself in each and every one? That's not unusual.

Because we are very human, and therefore very complex creatures, we all have a touch of these—and other—problems in our makeup; after all, a problem is a perfectly natural tendency that has gone wrong. It may have become exaggerated, or it may conflict with another perfectly natural tendency, or it may get suppressed for one reason or another.

So if you see yourself in all these problems, you may only be sensing your humanity. On the other hand, you may be recognizing some warning signals that will help you to prevent a natural tendency from becoming a problem.

But if you see that your life is handicapped in a way that matches one or some of the problems described—if these difficulties seem to be the obstacles to your inner satisfaction—then don't despair. First of all, you are aware, which means you have taken a step toward solving your problem. And, second, you live in a problem-solving, growth-inducing, body/mind-enhancing society, and you can choose any number of ways to get better.

Part 3
Helping Yourself

CHAPTER 24
A PERSONAL FIRST AID KIT

All of us, at some times in our lives, are touched by problems to some degree. Everyone has a sleepless night now and then, or an angry outburst caused by tension. Some of us smoke too much or have too many drinks when things go wrong. We have days when we're down in the dumps and experience self-doubt. We all have bad habits that are hard to break, and certain things that frighten us for no apparent reason. Sometimes we can't make up our minds, or we wish we could turn the clock back to a particularly wonderful time in the past. And who doesn't want to know more about how to reach his potential?

But notice: I said *to some degree*. Most of us get over these slumps within a short time and we're back to normal. Nevertheless, why put up with discomfort, even for a little while, when there is something you can do about it? And, by doing it, you can often prevent small discomforts from turning into big problems later on.

The following procedures are easy to do, require very little time, and most people who try them say they can be fun. Just remember, though, that they are recommended for minor disturbances and upsets. Real problems require professional therapy.

Perhaps you don't need a therapy or growth technique or body/mind technique for any specific difficulty. Or you might enjoy finding out about some of these methods, but you don't have the time right now. What you may need is a Personal First Aid Kit, something to pick you up when you feel down every now and then.

This Personal First Aid Kit is not something out of my own head. Nor is it a sample of methods developed and taught by the therapists and instructors discussed in Part I of this book. Rather, these exercises are a distillation of all the therapies, techniques, and trainings, but in a very simplified form which you can do by yourself.

Letting Go of Your Anger

Pounding the Pillow

You're angry and you're holding it in. Don't. Try this instead:

Find a room where you can be alone and can make noise without feeling self-conscious about it. Bring some pillows along with you.

Now, begin talking—out loud—about the way you feel. Don't hold back and don't be polite. Get as mad as you please. Raise your voice, shout, wave your arms, stamp your feet, swear. When you really begin to let go, pick up a pillow and begin punching it. Throw it across the room. Pick up another pillow and beat it up. Keep doing it until you begin to feel relaxed and relieved.

What you're doing is letting go of your anger, but in a situation that is under your control. You're not hurting anyone, but you're not stifling your feelings, and you're going to feel much better.

Shower Sobbing

You're so angry you could cry. Well, why don't you? Maybe you don't want anyone to see you crying. That's okay—you're entitled to privacy.

Go take a shower. Let the water run hard so that it makes a lot of noise—and let the tears come. Cry as hard as you please. No one will hear you above the noise of the water. And when you turn your face up into the spray of water, you'll feel as if the whole world is crying along with you—which, at a time like this, is kind of comforting.

The Empty Chair

Are you angry at someone and don't know why? Are you uncomfortable with your feelings?

You can get relief—and understanding—with this simplified version of a Gestalt technique:

Arrange two chairs facing each other and sit in one of them. Imagine the person causing your anger is sitting in the other chair.

Now begin to talk to the other person. Describe how you feel and try to explain why you feel angry. Then get up, sit in the empty chair, and "become" the other person. Respond to what you just said. Give the other person's side of the story.

Shift back to your chair and continue the dialogue, back and forth, always getting up and changing chairs to become one person or the other.

Gradually you will get beneath the apparent anger to the real cause of it. The "other person" is actually another facet of yourself, and as it begins to interrelate with the part of you that feels angry, it is able to bring your withheld emotions into your consciousness.

The important discovery here is not so much *why* you are angry, but why you can't let it out.

For Insomnia

A Wake-A-Thon

Can't sleep? You have to get up early in the morning and you have a big day ahead?

Then get up now. Don't try to sleep. Don't even allow yourself to sleep.

Get out of bed and into a comfortable chair. Read a book. Watch TV. Play solitaire. Bring your diary up to date. But no sleep allowed. Is that clear? All that tossing and turning and watching the clock—it's not for you. Stay up as late as you like. Enjoy yourself.

And before you know it—z-z-z-z-z. Or, if you don't actually fall asleep, you'll be relaxed. The point here is to reduce your anxiety about not sleeping and therefore make it easier to fall asleep.

Removing Communication Blocks

Repeat After Me

You and your friend have been misunderstanding each other lately. Maybe you both need to practice listening. Try this:

One of you tells the other what's bothering you. Do this without interruption. Then the other one tries to repeat what you said, but in her own words and without altering the meaning or emphasis. It isn't easy, and you may have to do it a few times. When it finally comes out right, reverse the process and you do the repeating.

This little exercise teaches each of you to listen to what the other one is *really* saying instead of hearing your own version of it. You'll be surprised at what a difference there can be.

Am I Hearing You Right?

This version of "Repeat After Me" is particularly effective with parents and teenagers. Let one person, parent or teenager, say what is on his mind, without interruption. Then the other person can say something such as: "Let me know if I'm hearing you right," and repeat what was said in his own words. The grammar isn't so great, but the logic is.

This I Like, That I Don't

The whole family can get into this act:

Set a time aside regularly when you all can get together, usually after a meal, when everyone is satisfied and relaxed.

Then allow each person one minute to say what she likes and doesn't like about the family. The appreciations don't have to equal the gripes necessarily, but there must be some of each. And no rebuttal or interruptions allowed!

The purpose is twofold: 1) Finding a reason to gripe is easy and it's good to get it out in the open rather than letting it build up into an outburst; 2) when you must find something to appreciate, you'll be amazed at how many good things you've been overlooking.

Meditation

Reaching into Yourself

There are many different ways to meditate, but most of them have a few things in common. How you breathe is very important. So is your ability to relax. A mantra is not absolutely necessary, but it may help to keep your mind from wandering.

Where you meditate matters. Choose a room where you won't be interrupted or distrcted by noise. Take your phone off the hook.

Some people meditate while lying down, but most people find a chair more effective, because when you're lying down, relaxed, it's too easy to fall asleep—and sleep isn't what meditation is all about.

Make yourself comfortable—which to some meditators means sitting upright with your spine unsupported by the chair, and to others means resting your spine against the back of the chair. Try each position and then decide which is better for you.

Don't rush into meditation. The first thing you have to do is relax, and that may take some time, depending upon how tense you are. Sit quietly for a while, or try "A Breathing Quickie" and "Countdown" techniques.

When you are relaxed and breathing slowly and evenly, close your eyes. If you have a mantra, now is the time to use it. If you don't have one, but would like to concentrate on something, use a pleasant-sounding word such as "peace," "good," "joy," "cosmos," or whatever appeals to your sense of serenity. Think the word slowly and keep repeating it as you breathe in and out.

Don't expect great things to happen. Meditation improves with practice, and in the beginning you may not get much out of it except a restful interval—which isn't bad. If your mind begins to wander, don't become irritable. Simply get back to where you were with your repeated word. If problems or disturbing thoughts come into your mind, don't wrestle with them. Acknowledge their presence and let them drift into and out of your consciousness.

Eventually you will feel detached from your body and physical surroundings. The word you are repeating will gradually fade from your awareness. You will be in touch with your higher or innermost self, deeply relaxed and thoroughly energized.

Now—to come back, begin repeating your word deliberately and slowly again. Be aware of your breathing. Be aware of your body, your posture, the chair you're sitting in. Open your eyes and see the room you are in.

Sit quietly for a moment, then stand up and stretch your arms toward the ceiling, clasping and unclasping your hands as if you were trying to grasp balloons off the ceiling.

Important: Meditation can be overdone to the point where you are *completely* cut off from your anxiety feelings, which is not good. Everyone needs a certain amount of stress in order to function well. So in the beginning, meditate for ten or fifteen minutes once or twice a day. Increase to twenty-minute sessions, no more than twice a day. Do not meditate just before going to bed, or you'll be too energized to sleep.

To Solve a Problem

Framing an Answer

If you can't find a solution to a problem, turn it over to your subconscious mind.

Sit in a chair and make yourself comfortable. Use one of the relaxation techniques that follow to relieve your tension, or try meditating.

Now, close your eyes and visualize your problem. Go over all the details in your mind. Mentally draw a blue frame around the image in your mind and mark a large X through the whole scene.

Next, imagine how you will feel when your problem is solved. Visualize the relief and joy of telling someone it is solved. Allow yourself to believe you have the solution within you. Then visualize a white frame around a black space. This is where your solution will appear. Watch it until you know what you must do to end your problem.

You may not get an answer the first time you try this technique. But try it again—and again. It works—provided, of course, that you really want to solve your problem. And if you don't, then that's another problem in itself, and one that may need professional therapy.

For Tension

Belly Breathing

Deep breathing is the basis for all yoga exercises, but "deep" is more than a long intake of air. Actually, a good yogic breath is done in three stages:

1. Lie on the floor and place your hands lightly on your belly. Let your belly stick up, completely relaxed, as far as it wants to go. (You may find this awkward at first, because, like most of us, you probably were taught to hold your belly in.)

Now begin to inhale. As air fills the bottom of your lungs, moving your diaphragm up and out, your belly will begin to flatten.

2. Continue inhaling and feel the lower part of your chest begin to swell. More air is moving into your lungs.

3. Finally the upper part of your chest—your rib section—swells. This means your lungs are completely filled with air. Hold your inhale for a moment, but don't become uncomfortable.

As you exhale, the process is reversed. Your chest begins to flatten and your belly becomes round again.

At first it's best to be conscious of the changes in your body as you inhale and exhale, but with practice you can breathe deeply yet smoothly and easily.

Do this six times at first. Then increase to eight, ten, a dozen deep breaths a day to prevent as well as relieve tension.

Countdown

Before meditating, before going to sleep, or simply when you'd like to relax, try this:

Lie on the floor or in bed, or sit in a comfortable chair. Keep your hands at your sides, or let them rest on the arms of your chair.

Beginning with your toes and going all the way up to your face (and even your scalp), visualize each part of your body attaining a state of relaxation. If you meet resistance, concentrate on that part of your body and tell it to relax. Take your time. Go back over any area that becomes tense again until finally your whole body is relaxed.

A Breathing Quickie

You can do this just about anywhere when you feel panicky: Standing, sitting, or walking, alone or in a group, breathe in and out deeply, slowly, with your mouth closed, for about three minutes. You'll feel calmer.

For Better Sex

That Feels Good

You're trying so hard to have an orgasm that very often you can't? Believe me, you're not alone.

You and your sex partner need to get out from under the pressure, so the next time you make love, try something different:

First, agree that you won't have sex—but you will have sexuality. And sensitivity. That means you'll stop short of intercourse, but you'll touch, kiss, massage, nibble, cuddle, explore, and do anything else that feels absolutely delicious.

Second, agree to tell each other what feels good and what you would like each other to do.

Now, let the man assume a comfortable sitting position with the woman sitting in front of him and leaning back against his chest. (Just the leisurely sensation of one body against the other can be delightful.)

With the woman directing him, the man begins to move his hands along her body, stimulating areas that give her specific pleasure, but avoiding the more familiar genital area, because, as you both agreed, no sex. You'll be amazed at how many new and excitable erogenous areas you will find.

The purpose here is to awaken a woman to the many ways in which her body can give her pleasure, and to make a man more aware that there is more than one way to stimulate her.

Take your time. Remember to tell each other—and ask each other—what feels good.

After a while you both may feel so wonderfully aroused that you may regret you agreed not to go all the way. In which case, it's okay to cheat.

Room to Move

A woman gets tired of the same old position, and she deserves a change. Let her get on top, where she can move around instead of feeling pinned down all the time. A man likes variety, too.

One of the most enjoyable positions for a woman is to lie on top of the man at a thirty-degree angle, with her left leg bent at the knee and outside the man's extended right leg. Her right leg is extended along his bent left leg, her right thigh resting on his left thigh. As she raises and lowers herself, most of her weight is on her left knee.

Most sex therapists recommend this position for increased enjoyment for both partners, even when there are no specific problems.

Getting in Touch with Your Feelings

A Dream Diary

You can't psychoanalyze your dreams. That takes professional expertise. But you can train yourself to remember more of your dreams, and you can understand some of the little clues they offer to help you deal with everyday situations.

1. Before you go to sleep, tell yourself you are going to remember your dreams.

2. Put a pad and pencil by your bed.

3. As soon as you wake up, write down everything you can remember about your dreams. At first you may not remember much at all, but with practice your memory will improve.

4. Pay attention to the emotions expressed in your dreams: the frustration you feel when you're running and getting nowhere, the fear you experience in dark places, your anxiety over losing your way or being late for an appointment. These feelings are real and the dreams are trying to bring them to

your attention. Once you realize what they are, you can do something about them.

For Depression

How Bad It Is!

We all get moments when we feel absolutely miserable, hopeless, insecure, and discouraged. So the next time it happens to you, don't fight it. That's right, I said *don't.*

Instead, revel in your depression. Think about how rotten you feel. Think about it in great detail. Talk to yourself about it, and offer yourself plenty of sympathy. Try to convince yourself that you're more depressed than anyone you know. In fact, proclaim that you're the most miserable person in the whole world. *Insist* on it.

And if you don't start laughing at yourself by this time, then you *do* have a problem.

The idea here is to be open about your desire for sympathy, and once you realize that sympathy is what you're after, you can get some perspective on your gloom.

A variation of this method works beautifully with more than one person, assuming, of course, that you all understand the reason behind it. Let each person describe how awful he feels, and before you know it, each one of you will be competing for the title of Most Depressed Person—until you realize what you're doing and begin to laugh at yourselves.

Weeding Your Garden

When you feel as if the whole world has gone wrong, a little yoga may help:

Sit cross-legged on the floor, hands resting in your lap and palms up. Breathe slowly and carefully, making sure you hold both the inhale and exhale. When your breathing becomes regular and rhythmic, begin meditating, using a mantra to help you concentrate. As you reach the deeper levels of your consciousness, begin to go through your thoughts as if you were a gardener weeding out a seedbed. See yourself uprooting the negative thoughts and fertilizing the positive ones.

This technique also is effective for overcoming your fears.

The Cookie

You may have been holding up very well under a prolonged strain—such as caring for a new baby, losing your job, starting your own business, moving to another part of the country, taking exams, or whatever—but you're beginning to get a bit depressed lately.

Naturally. You've had to be an Adult all this time, and your Natural Child feels neglected. You can't stop what you're doing to have a good time, but you can give the Child a cookie to brighten her spirits and let her know you care.

Do something that you enjoyed as a child. Buy yourself an ice cream cone and lick it up. Go to a funny movie. Play with your dog. Take time out for a few sets of tennis with a friend. Go swimming or take a walk in the country. Go sleigh riding on a snowy day. Visit the zoo. Watch a parade. Go to the circus. Read a sexy novel.

If you give your Child a cookie to tide her through the time of strain, she'll soon stop pouting and you'll feel much brighter.

Making a Decision

Sleep-Solving

Can't make up your mind what to do? Maybe you can get some help from your dreams.

Before going to bed, think about your choices. Don't even try to decide between them at this point, because you'll only become tense. Right now your goal is to get your subconscious mind to work for you, so just allow the choices to present themselves clearly in your mind.

Tell yourself that you are going to make your decision while you sleep. Then relax and go to sleep.

You may not have the decision the next morning, or the next few mornings, but if you keep trying, one morning you will awake with your mind made up.

Try this technique when you are having trouble solving a problem. I know an artist who programs his subconscious mind to come up with new designs while he sleeps.

A Present for a Parent

Sometimes you can't decide to do something because it goes against the way your parents did it. You don't want your Critical Parent nagging you, so you stall and find excuses to avoid making your decision.

There's a way out. Give your Parent token compliance, and then go your own way.

For instance, if you really want to have your own apartment, but your Critical Parent makes you feel guilty about moving out of the homestead, try sharing an apartment with a friend as a start. Have dinner once a week with your parents.

And If I Don't?

Can't choose between your alternatives?

Sit down with pencil and paper and begin making two lists: one, your options, and the other, the consequences of each. You say you've tried that before and it didn't work? Be patient. This is different.

Now consider the fact that you have a third option. That's right. If you *don't* make a decision, that's a decision in itself, and it also has consequences. So pick up your pencil and make a third list: What will happen if you don't choose one alternative over the other?

Once you realize that *something* is going to happen whether you decide or not, you will usually find a decision easier to make.

Say Ah-h-h-h!

As you use these exercises to relieve you of occasional tension, frustration, and emotional discomfort, as you allow them to improve your physical well-being and clear your mind for better thinking, you will notice a difference in your life. Even a little pollution can upset the balance of your inner ecology, and once the balance is restored, you will function better in body, mind, and spirit.

It will be like saying a great, big *ah-h-h-h!* inside yourself. And you can just imagine how good that will feel.

APPENDIX: WHERE TO GO FOR HELP

Therapies

Behavior Modification Therapy: Inquire at local hospital, university, or mental health center.

Gestalt Therapy:

Mrs. Laura Perls
Gestalt Therapy Institute
7 West 96 Street
New York, NY 10015

Gestalt Institute of San Francisco
1719 Union Street
San Francisco, CA 94123

Boulder Workshop
2889 Valmont Road
Boulder, CO 80301

Gestalt Center for Psychotherapy
7200 Cresheim Road
Philadelphia, PA 19118

Gestalt Institute of Canada
P.O. Box 39
Lake Cowichan
British Columbia
Canada

Group Therapy: Inquire at local hospital, university, or mental health center. Also:

Encounter Consultants
P.O. Box 1455
Cody, Wyoming 92414

Encounters
The Huntington, Suite 209
5225 Connecticut Avenue, NW
Washington, D.C. 20015

Esalen/Big Sur
Big Sur, CA 93920

Esalen/San Francisco
1793 Union Street
San Francisco, CA 94123

Family Group Institute
649 Irving Street
San Francisco, CA 94122

Human Growth Center
376 Broadway
Arcade Building
Saratoga Springs, NY 12866

National Training
Laboratories
Bethel, ME 04217

Hypnotherapy:

National Academy of
Medical Hypnosis
300 Interstate North, NW
Atlanta, GA 30339

New York Psychoanalytic
Institute
245 East 82 Street
New York, NY 10028

Primal Scream Therapy:

Center for the Whole Person
304 West 105 Street
New York, NY 10025

Dr. Arthur Janov
620 N. Almont
Los Angeles, CA 90032

The Clearing
P.O. Box 835
San Rafael, CA 94902

Psychoanalytic Therapy: Inquire at local hospital, university, or mental health center; ask physician, minister, social worker. Also:

Institute of Psychoanalysis
186 Second Avenue
New York, NY 10003

New York Psychoanalytic
Institute
245 East 82 Street
New York, NY 10028

Sex Therapy:

Anew
537 Charles Lane
Mill Valley, CA 94941

Center for Social and
Sensory Learning
6350 De Longspre
Los Angeles, CA 90028

Van Hamett Clinic
Hahnemann College of
Medicine
314 North Broad Street
Philadelphia, PA 19102

Transactional Analysis:

International Transactional Analysis Association
1771 Vallejo Street
San Francisco, CA 94123

Growth Techniques

Arica:

Arica Institute
24 West 57 Street
New York, NY 10019

Assertiveness Training: Inquire at local hospital, university, or mental health center.

Silva Mind Control:

Silva Mind Control International
1110 Cedar, Box 1415
Laredo, TX 78040

Silva Mind Control of New England
Suite 24
53 Paul Street
Newton Center, MA 02159

Transcendental Meditation: Contact your local International Meditation Society chapter.

Body/Mind Techniques

Bioenergetics:

Institute of Bioenergetic Analysis
144 East 36 Street
New York, NY 10016

Biofeedback:

Biofeedback Society
University of Colorado
Denver, CO 80202

Rolfing:

Rolf Institute of Structural Integration
P.O. Box 1868
Boulder, CO 80302

Yoga: Watch your local newspapers for announcements of yoga classes. Also:

A'nanda Ma'rga
North America Sectorial Headquarters
854 Pearl Street
Denver, CO 80203

Ananda Meditation Village
Ananda Cooperative Village
Allegheny Star Route
Nevada City, CA 95959

Aquarian Age Yoga Center
620 14 Street
Virginia Beach, VA 23451

Integral Yoga Institute
Satchidananda Ashram
P.O. Box 108
Pomfret Center, CT 06259

est: Contact est centers in major cities. Also:

est
765 California Street
San Francisco, CA 94108

INDEX